SU
MASTERY

Everything You Need to Launch, Operate, and Grow Your Newsletter Empire

The Ultimate Guide for Aspiring Newsletter Business Entrepreneurs

Robert C Tilford

Copyright © 2024 by Robert C Tilford

All rights reserved. No part of this publication may be reproduced, distributed, or transmitted in any form or by any means, including photocopying, recording, or other electronic or mechanical methods, without the prior written permission of the publisher, except in the case of brief quotations embodied in critical reviews and certain other noncommercial uses permitted by copyright law.

Published by:

Robert C Tilford

The information contained in this book is for educational and informational purposes only and is not intended as financial, legal, or tax advice. Please consult a qualified professional for specific advice tailored to your individual situation.

The author and publisher have made every effort to ensure the accuracy and completeness of the information contained in this book but assume no responsibility for errors, inaccuracies, omissions, or any inconsistency herein. Any slights of people, places, or organizations are unintentional.

Trademark Disclaimer: All trademarks, service marks, and trade names mentioned in this book are the property of their respective owners and are used for identification purposes only. Use of these marks does not imply endorsement or affiliation.

Table of Contents

Introduction 7

Chapter 1: Getting Started with Substack 13
- 1.1 What is Substack? 13
- 1.2 Setting Up Your Substack Account 20
- 1.3 Initial Configuration 28

Chapter 2: Defining Your Niche and Value Proposition 37
- 2.1 Importance of Niche Selection 37
- 2.2 How to Choose a Niche 43
- 2.3 Understanding Your Audience 50
- 2.4 Crafting Your Value Proposition 58

Chapter 3: Crafting Engaging Content 67
- 3.1 Content Strategy Basics 67
- 3.2 Editorial Calendar 76
- 3.3 Types of Content 83
- 3.4 Writing Tips and Best Practices 92

Chapter 4: Designing Your Newsletter 101
- 4.1 Selecting a Template 101
- 4.2 Customizing Your Header 107
- 4.3 Typography and Readability Tips 112
- 4.4 Using Visual Elements Effectively 117
- 4.5 Creating a Professional and Appealing Layout 122

Chapter 5: Building and Engaging Your Audience 127
- 5.1 Initial Promotion Strategies 127
- 5.2 Leveraging Social Media 132

5.3 Optimizing for Search Engines 138

5.4 Building a Community Around Your Newsletter 143

5.5 Using Substack's Community Features 147

5.6 Creating a Feedback Loop 153

Chapter 6: Monetization Strategies **159**

6.1 Free vs. Paid Subscriptions 159

6.2 Offering Tiered Subscriptions 164

6.3 Finding Sponsors and Creating Sponsored Content 169

6.4 Affiliate Marketing 175

6.5 Additional Revenue Streams 179

Chapter 7: Advanced Growth Tactics **187**

7.1 Cross-Promotion with Other Newsletters 187

7.2 Utilizing Substack's Recommendation Feature 192

7.3 Running Referral Programs 198

7.4 Analyzing and Optimizing Performance 203

7.5 Conducting A/B Testing 208

Chapter 8: Daily Operations and Management **215**

8.1 Content Creation Workflow 215

8.2 Managing Subscriber Interactions 220

8.3 Performance Tracking 225

8.4 Essential Tools for Content Management 229

8.5 Payment Processing and Financial Management 233

8.6 Legal and Administrative Considerations 238

Chapter 9: Case Studies and Expert Insights **243**

9.1 Detailed Case Studies of Successful Substack Newsletters 243

9.2 Insights from Top Substack Creators 248

Conclusion **253**
Appendix A: Glossary of Terms **257**
Appendix B: Templates and Checklists **261**
    Content Planning Template 261
    Newsletter Launch Checklist 262
    Weekly Newsletter Management Checklist 263
    Sponsored Content Checklist 264
    Monthly Performance Review Template 265
Appendix C: Additional Resources and Reading **267**
    Recommended Books 267
    Recommended Articles 267
    Online Resources and Tools 268
    Online Communities and Forums 269

Introduction

Why Substack?

In the ever-evolving landscape of digital media, one platform has emerged as a game-changer for content creators, writers, and entrepreneurs alike: Substack. But why Substack? What makes it the go-to platform for launching and growing a successful newsletter business?

Substack offers a unique blend of simplicity and power. It allows you to focus on what you do best—creating compelling content—while handling the technical complexities of email delivery, payment processing, and audience management. Whether you're a seasoned writer looking to monetize your expertise or a budding entrepreneur eager to build a loyal audience, Substack provides the tools and support you need to succeed.

The Rise of Newsletters

Newsletters have experienced a renaissance in recent years. Once considered a relic of the early internet, they have now become a vital channel for direct, personal communication with audiences. Unlike social media platforms, where algorithms dictate who sees your content, newsletters offer a direct line to your readers' inboxes. This direct connection fosters a sense of intimacy and trust that is hard to achieve elsewhere.

The resurgence of newsletters can be attributed to several factors. First, there's the growing fatigue with social media's noise and distractions. Readers are seeking more meaningful, curated content delivered straight to them. Second, newsletters offer creators a sustainable business model. With the right strategies, you can turn your passion for writing into a profitable venture, free from the whims of ad revenue and platform changes.

Benefits of Using Substack

Substack stands out in the crowded field of newsletter platforms for several reasons:

1. **Ease of Use:** Substack's user-friendly interface makes it easy to get started, even if you're not tech-savvy. You can set up your newsletter, customize your profile, and start publishing in minutes.

2. **Monetization Options:** Substack offers robust monetization features, including paid subscriptions, tiered memberships, and the ability to offer subscriber-only content. This flexibility allows you to tailor your revenue model to your audience's preferences.

3. **Community Features:** Substack isn't just a publishing platform; it's a community. With features like discussion threads and recommendations, you can engage with your readers and build a loyal following.

4. **Analytics and Insights:** Substack provides detailed analytics to help you understand your audience and optimize your content. From open rates to subscriber growth, you have the data you need to make informed decisions.

Success Stories

The proof of Substack's potential lies in the success stories of its creators. Take, for example, Casey Newton, who left his job at The Verge to launch Platformer on Substack. Within months, he had thousands of paying subscribers and a thriving community. Or consider Emily Atkin, whose climate-focused newsletter Heated has not only garnered a substantial readership but also influenced public discourse on environmental issues.

These success stories are not outliers. They are a testament to the power of Substack as a platform for independent creators. With the right approach, you too can build a successful newsletter business that resonates with your audience and generates sustainable income.

What to Expect from This Book

"Substack Mastery: Everything You Need to Launch, Operate, and Grow Your Newsletter Empire" is your comprehensive guide to navigating the world of Substack. Whether you're just starting or looking to take your newsletter to the next level, this book covers everything you need to know.

We'll start with the basics, guiding you through setting up your Substack account and configuring your initial settings. From there, we'll delve into the critical aspects of defining your niche and crafting a compelling value proposition. You'll learn how to create engaging content, design a visually appealing newsletter, and build a loyal audience.

But we won't stop there. This book also covers advanced growth tactics, monetization strategies, and the daily operations of running a successful newsletter business. You'll gain insights from detailed case studies and expert interviews, providing you with real-world examples and actionable advice.

Our Promise to You

Our goal with this book is simple: to empower you with the knowledge and tools you need to succeed on Substack. We believe that everyone has a unique voice and valuable insights to share.

With Substack, you have the opportunity to turn your passion into a thriving business.

So, whether you're a writer, journalist, entrepreneur, or simply someone with a story to tell, this book is for you. Let's embark on this journey together and unlock the full potential of your newsletter empire.

Welcome to "Substack Mastery." Let's get started.

Chapter 1: Getting Started with Substack

1.1 What is Substack?

In the ever-evolving landscape of digital content creation, Substack has emerged as a game-changer for writers, journalists, and entrepreneurs alike. It's a platform that empowers content creators to publish directly to their audience, build a loyal following, and monetize their work. But what exactly sets Substack apart from the myriad of other content platforms out there? Let's dive in and explore the essence of Substack.

The Substack Revolution

At its core, Substack is a platform that combines the simplicity of email with the power of a blog. It allows you to create, distribute, and monetize newsletters effortlessly. But Substack is more than just a tool; it represents a shift in the way content creators approach their craft. It puts you, the creator, in the driver's seat. You own your content, your mailing list, and your revenue streams. This level of autonomy is a breath of fresh air in an industry often dominated by gatekeepers and algorithms.

Substack was founded in 2017 by Chris Best, Hamish McKenzie, and Jairaj Sethi, three individuals who shared a vision of empowering writers to go independent and thrive. Their mission was clear: to provide a platform that would allow creators to focus on what they do best—creating compelling content—while taking care of the technical complexities behind the scenes. And boy, did they deliver!

Since its inception, Substack has grown by leaps and bounds, attracting a diverse range of creators, from established journalists to passionate hobbyists. The platform's success can be attributed to its user-friendly interface, robust feature set, and unwavering commitment to putting creators first.

The Power of Substack: Key Features and Benefits

So, what makes Substack tick? Let's take a closer look at some of the key features and benefits that have made it the go-to platform for content creators worldwide.

1. Simplicity at Its Finest

One of the most significant advantages of Substack is its simplicity. You don't need to be a tech wizard to get started. The platform guides you through the setup process with ease, from creating your account to publishing your first post. The intuitive dashboard makes managing your content, subscribers, and revenue a breeze. Substack's user-friendly interface allows you to focus on what truly matters: creating exceptional content.

2. Seamless Monetization

Monetizing your content on Substack is a piece of cake. The platform seamlessly integrates with Stripe, a leading payment processor, to handle subscriptions and payments. This integration enables you to offer paid subscriptions, tiered memberships, and one time payments without breaking a sweat. Say goodbye to the hassle of setting up complex payment systems and hello to a streamlined monetization process.

3. Customization is Key

While Substack prioritizes simplicity, it doesn't compromise on customization. You have the freedom to create a newsletter that reflects your unique brand. Choose from a variety of templates, customize your header, and incorporate your branding elements to make your newsletter stand out from the crowd. Substack understands that your newsletter is an extension of your identity, and it provides the tools to make it truly yours.

4. Building a Thriving Community

Substack is more than just a publishing platform; it's a community hub. With features like discussion threads and subscriber-only content, you can foster meaningful interactions with your readers and build a loyal following. These engagement tools create a sense of belonging and encourage reader participation, which is the lifeblood of any successful newsletter.

5. Data-Driven Insights

To create content that resonates with your audience, you need to understand them. Substack provides comprehensive analytics, including open rates, subscriber growth, and revenue metrics. These insights give you a pulse on your newsletter's performance, allowing you to make informed decisions and fine-tune your content strategy. With Substack, you have the data at your fingertips to optimize your newsletter and keep your readers coming back for more.

Substack vs. The Competition

In the crowded world of content platforms, it's essential to understand how Substack stacks up against its competitors. Let's take a quick look at some popular alternatives and highlight where Substack shines.

1. Mailchimp: The Email Marketing Behemoth

Mailchimp is a well-established email marketing platform that offers a wide range of features for creating and managing newsletters. While it provides extensive customization options and advanced marketing tools, it can be overwhelming for beginners. Substack, on the other hand, offers a more streamlined and user-friendly experience, making it the perfect choice for writers who want to focus on their craft without getting bogged down in technical complexities.

2. Medium: The Blogging Platform

Medium is a popular blogging platform that allows writers to publish articles and reach a broad audience. While it offers the potential for viral reach and a built-in audience, it lacks the direct monetization options that Substack provides. With Substack, you have the power to build a direct relationship with your readers and monetize your content through subscriptions, giving you greater control over your income.

3. Patreon: The Membership Platform

Patreon is a membership platform that enables creators to earn money from their fans through subscriptions. While it offers robust membership features, it caters to a wide range of content types, such as videos, podcasts, and art. Substack, on the other hand, is tailored specifically for writers and newsletter creators, providing a focused and streamlined experience.

Why Choose Substack? The Bottom Line

With so many platforms vying for your attention, why should you choose Substack for your newsletter business? Here are a few compelling reasons:

1. Ownership and Control

On Substack, you are the master of your domain. You own your content, your mailing list, and your revenue streams. This level of ownership is crucial for building a sustainable business. Unlike social media platforms, where algorithms dictate your reach, Substack allows you to communicate directly with your audience on your own terms.

2. Flexibility in Monetization

Substack offers a range of monetization options to suit your needs. Whether you prefer to offer free subscriptions, paid subscriptions, tiered memberships, or one-time payments, Substack has you covered. This flexibility allows you to tailor your revenue model to your audience's preferences and maximize your earning potential.

3. Community Building Made Easy

Building a loyal community around your newsletter is essential for long-term success. Substack's community features, such as discussion threads and subscriber-only content, provide the tools to engage with your readers and foster a sense of belonging. By nurturing a thriving community, you can create a dedicated fan base that will support you every step of the way.

4. Simplicity and Ease of Use

Substack's user-friendly interface and straightforward setup process make it accessible to everyone, regardless of technical expertise. The platform takes care of the nitty-gritty details, such as email delivery, payment processing, and audience management, allowing you to focus on what you do best: creating exceptional content.

- Substack is more than just a newsletter platform; it's a catalyst for change in the world of content creation. It empowers writers, journalists, and entrepreneurs to take control of their content, build direct relationships with their audience, and monetize their work on their own terms. With its user-friendly interface, robust feature set, and commitment to creator autonomy, Substack is the ultimate tool for launching and growing a successful newsletter business.

In the upcoming sections, we'll guide you through the process of setting up your Substack account, customizing your profile, and configuring your initial settings. By the end of this chapter, you'll be well-equipped to embark on your Substack journey and start building the newsletter empire of your dreams. So, buckle up and get ready to dive into the exciting world of Substack!

1.2 Setting Up Your Substack Account

Now that you have a solid understanding of what Substack is and how it can benefit your newsletter business, it's time to dive into the practical steps of setting up your account. In this section, we'll walk you through the process of creating your Substack account, customizing your profile, choosing a name and URL, and setting up your domain. By the end of this section, you'll be ready to start building your newsletter empire on Substack.

Creating an Account

The first step in your Substack journey is creating an account. Fortunately, Substack makes this process incredibly simple and straightforward. To get started, head over to the Substack website (https://substack.com) and click on the "Start Writing" button in the top-right corner of the page.

You'll be prompted to enter your email address and create a password. Alternatively, you can sign up using your Google or X (formerly Twitter) account, which can save you some time and streamline the process. Once you've entered your information, click on the "Create Account" button, and voila! You're officially a member of the Substack community.

Customizing Your Profile

With your account created, it's time to customize your profile and make it truly yours. Your profile is the first thing potential subscribers will see when they visit your Substack page, so it's essential to make a great first impression. Substack provides a range of customization options to help you create a profile that reflects your brand and personality.

To access your profile settings, click on your profile icon in the top-right corner of the Substack dashboard and select "Settings" from the dropdown menu. From there, navigate to the "Profile" tab, where you'll find a variety of fields to fill out and customize.

1. Profile Picture

Your profile picture is a crucial element of your Substack identity. It's the first visual representation of you and your brand that potential subscribers will encounter. Choose a high-quality image that reflects your personality and the tone of your newsletter. This could be a professional headshot, a logo, or an eye-catching graphic that aligns with your niche.

To upload your profile picture, simply click on the "Upload Image" button and select the desired image from your computer. Substack recommends using an image with a minimum size of 256x256 pixels for optimal clarity and resolution.

2. Display Name

Your display name is the name that will appear on your Substack page and in your newsletter emails. It can be your real name, a pen name, or a brand name, depending on your preference and the nature of your newsletter. Choose a name that is memorable, easy to pronounce, and aligns with your niche and target audience.

To set your display name, simply type it into the "Display Name" field in your profile settings.

3. Bio

Your bio is a short description of who you are and what your newsletter is about. It's an opportunity to showcase your expertise, personality, and unique value proposition. Use this space to give potential subscribers a compelling reason to sign up for your newsletter.

When crafting your bio, keep it concise, engaging, and informative. Highlight your relevant experience, credentials, and achievements, and give readers a taste of what they can expect from your newsletter. Don't be afraid to inject some personality and humor into your bio to make it more memorable and relatable.

To add your bio, simply type it into the "Bio" field in your profile settings. Substack allows you to use basic formatting, such as bold, italic, and hyperlinks, to make your bio more visually appealing and interactive.

4. Social Media Links

Substack allows you to link your social media profiles to your Substack page, making it easy for subscribers to connect with you on other platforms. This is a great way to expand your reach, engage with your audience, and drive traffic back to your newsletter.

To add your social media links, scroll down to the "Social Media" section in your profile settings. You'll see fields for X (formerly Twitter), Facebook, Instagram, LinkedIn, and YouTube. Simply enter the URLs for your respective profiles, and Substack will automatically display the corresponding icons on your page.

Choosing a Name and URL

Now that you've customized your profile, it's time to choose a name and URL for your newsletter. This is a crucial step, as your name and URL will be the primary identifiers of your newsletter across the web. It's essential to choose a name and URL that are memorable, relevant, and aligned with your brand and niche.

1. Newsletter Name

Your newsletter name should be catchy, descriptive, and reflective of your content and personality. It should give potential subscribers a clear idea of what your newsletter is about and what value it provides. Consider using keywords related to your niche to make your name more searchable and discoverable.

Some tips for choosing a great newsletter name:

Keep it short and sweet: Aim for a name that is easy to remember and type.

Use alliteration or rhyme: Catchy names that incorporate alliteration or rhyme can be more memorable and engaging.

Avoid generic names: Choose a name that sets you apart from other newsletters in your niche.

Consider your target audience: Select a name that resonates with your ideal subscribers and reflects their interests and preferences.

To set your newsletter name, navigate to the "Publication" tab in your Substack settings and enter your desired name in the "Publication Name" field.

2. URL

Your Substack URL is the web address that subscribers will use to access your newsletter page. By default, Substack assigns you a URL based on your newsletter name, but you have the option to customize it to make it more branded and memorable.

When choosing your URL, keep the following tips in mind:

Keep it short and simple: Aim for a URL that is easy to remember and type.

Use your brand name: If you have an established brand or personal name, consider incorporating it into your URL for consistency and recognition.

Avoid hyphens and underscores: Hyphens and underscores can make your URL harder to remember and type, so it's best to avoid them if possible.

Consider your niche: If your newsletter focuses on a specific topic or keyword, consider incorporating it into your URL for better searchability and discoverability.

To customize your URL, navigate to the "Publication" tab in your Substack settings and click on the "Edit" button next to your current URL. Enter your desired URL and click "Save" to update it.

Setting Up Your Domain

While Substack provides you with a default URL, you also have the option to use your own custom domain for your newsletter. Using a custom domain can help you establish a stronger brand identity, improve your credibility, and make your newsletter more memorable and professional.

To set up a custom domain on Substack, you'll need to purchase a domain from a domain registrar such as GoDaddy, Namecheap, or Google Domains. Once you have your domain, follow these steps to connect it to your Substack account:

1. Navigate to the "Settings" tab in your Substack dashboard and click on the "Custom Domain" option.

2. Enter your custom domain in the "Domain" field and click "Continue."

3. Substack will provide you with a set of DNS records that you'll need to add to your domain registrar's settings. These records typically include an A record, CNAME record, and MX records.

4. Log in to your domain registrar's account and navigate to the DNS settings for your domain.

5. Add the DNS records provided by Substack, making sure to copy them exactly as they appear.

6. Save your changes and wait for the DNS propagation to complete. This process can take up to 48 hours, but it usually happens much faster.

7. Once the DNS propagation is complete, return to your Substack settings and click on the "Verify Domain" button to confirm that your custom domain is properly connected.

Using a custom domain not only enhances your brand identity but also gives you more control over your newsletter's online presence. It can also make it easier for subscribers to remember and share your newsletter URL, potentially leading to increased traffic and engagement.

- Setting up your Substack account is a crucial first step in launching your newsletter business. By customizing your profile, choosing a memorable name and URL, and optionally setting up a custom domain, you'll be well on your way to establishing a strong brand identity and attracting subscribers.

In the next section, we'll dive into the initial configuration of your Substack account, including basic settings, social media integration, and setting up your first post. Stay tuned for more practical tips and guidance on how to set your newsletter up for success from the very beginning.

1.3 Initial Configuration

With your Substack account set up and your profile customized, it's time to dive into the initial configuration of your newsletter. This section will guide you through the essential settings, social media integration, and the process of setting up your first post. By the end of this section, you'll have a solid foundation for your Substack newsletter and be ready to start creating content.

Basic Settings

Substack offers a range of basic settings that allow you to customize your newsletter's functionality and appearance. To access these settings, navigate to the "Settings" tab in your Substack dashboard.

1. Publication Settings

The "Publication" tab is where you can manage your newsletter's core settings, such as your publication name, description, and URL. You can also set your newsletter's language, time zone, and default post visibility (public or paid subscribers only).

Take some time to review these settings and ensure they align with your brand and goals. Your publication description, in particular, is an important element, as it appears on your Substack page and helps potential subscribers understand what your newsletter is about.

2. Email Settings

The "Email" tab is where you can configure your newsletter's email settings, such as your sender name, reply-to address, and email footer. You can also customize your email template, choosing from a selection of pre-designed templates or creating your own using HTML and CSS.

When setting up your email settings, consider the following best practices:

Use a clear and recognizable sender name that includes your name or brand.

Set a reply-to address that you regularly monitor, so you can easily engage with subscribers who respond to your emails.

Customize your email footer to include your contact information, social media links, and any necessary legal disclaimers.

Choose an email template that aligns with your brand and provides a clean, readable layout for your content.

3. Subscription Settings

The "Subscription" tab is where you can manage your newsletter's subscription settings, such as your pricing, payment methods, and subscription tiers. If you plan to offer paid subscriptions, this is where you'll set up your payment processor (Stripe) and configure your subscription options.

When setting up your subscription settings, consider the following factors:

Your pricing strategy: Will you offer a free subscription, a paid subscription, or a combination of both? If you offer paid subscriptions, consider your target audience and the value you provide to determine a fair and competitive price point.

Your subscription tiers: Will you offer multiple subscription tiers with different levels of access or benefits? Tiers can be a great way to provide options for your subscribers and increase your revenue potential.

Your payment processor: Substack currently integrates with Stripe for payment processing. You'll need to set up a Stripe account and connect it to your Substack account to enable paid subscriptions.

4. Analytics Settings

The "Analytics" tab is where you can view your newsletter's performance metrics, such as your subscriber growth, open rates, and click rates. You can also integrate with third-party analytics tools, such as Google Analytics, to gain deeper insights into your audience and content performance.

When setting up your analytics, consider the following tips:

Set up Google Analytics: Integrating Google Analytics with your Substack account can provide valuable insights into your website traffic, audience demographics, and content engagement.

Monitor your key metrics: Regularly review your subscriber growth, open rates, and click rates to identify trends and optimize your content and marketing strategies.

Use analytics to inform your decisions: Let your analytics guide your content planning, promotional efforts, and subscriber engagement strategies. Continuously test and refine your approach based on your data.

Integrating Social Media

Integrating your social media accounts with your Substack newsletter can help you expand your reach, engage with your audience, and drive traffic to your newsletter. Substack allows you to connect your X (formerly Twitter), Facebook, and Instagram accounts, making it easy for subscribers to follow you on other platforms.

To integrate your social media accounts, navigate to the "Profile" tab in your Substack settings and scroll down to the "Social Media" section. Here, you can enter the URLs for your X (formerly Twitter), Facebook, and Instagram profiles.

Once you've connected your social media accounts, they will appear as icons on your Substack page, allowing subscribers to easily follow you on their preferred platforms. Additionally, Substack automatically generates social media share buttons for your newsletter posts, making it easy for readers to share your content with their own followers.

When integrating social media with your Substack newsletter, consider the following best practices:

Choose the right platforms: Focus on the social media platforms where your target audience is most active and engaged. You don't need to be on every platform – choose the ones that align with your niche and goals.

Create platform-specific content: While you can certainly share your newsletter posts on social media, also consider creating platform-specific content that complements your newsletter and engages your followers in different ways.

Engage with your followers: Don't just broadcast your content on social media – take the time to engage with your followers, respond to comments and messages, and build relationships with your audience.

Use social media to drive newsletter subscriptions: Regularly promote your newsletter on your social media channels, highlighting the value and benefits of subscribing. Consider offering exclusive content or incentives to encourage social media followers to sign up for your newsletter.

Setting Up Your First Post

With your basic settings and social media integration in place, it's time to set up your first Substack post. This initial post is an opportunity to introduce yourself, your newsletter, and your value proposition to your subscribers.

To create your first post, click on the "New Post" button in the top-right corner of your Substack dashboard. This will open the post editor, where you can write your content, add images and multimedia, and configure your post settings.

When crafting your first post, consider the following tips:

Start with a strong headline: Your headline should be attention-grabbing, informative, and reflective of your newsletter's value proposition. Use strong, active language and consider including keywords related to your niche.

Introduce yourself and your newsletter: Use your first post to introduce yourself, your background, and your expertise. Explain why you started your newsletter, what topics you'll cover, and what value you aim to provide to your subscribers.

Set expectations: Clearly communicate what subscribers can expect from your newsletter, including the types of content you'll publish, the frequency of your emails, and any special features or benefits you offer.

Showcase your writing style: Your first post should give readers a taste of your writing style and personality. Write in a way that is engaging, informative, and reflective of your brand voice.

Include a call-to-action: End your first post with a clear call-to-action, encouraging readers to subscribe to your newsletter, follow you on social media, or take another desired action.

Once you've written your first post, take some time to review and edit it for clarity, grammar, and style. When you're ready to publish, click the "Publish" button in the top-right corner of the post editor.

After publishing your first post, take a moment to promote it on your social media channels and to your existing network. This initial promotion can help you attract your first subscribers and generate buzz around your newsletter launch.

Configuring your Substack settings, integrating social media, and setting up your first post are essential steps in launching your newsletter. By taking the time to carefully consider your settings, create a strong social media presence, and craft an engaging first post, you'll set yourself up for success as you begin your Substack journey.

In the next chapter, we'll dive into the crucial topic of defining your niche and crafting your value proposition. This foundational work will guide your content creation, marketing efforts, and overall strategy as you grow your newsletter business.

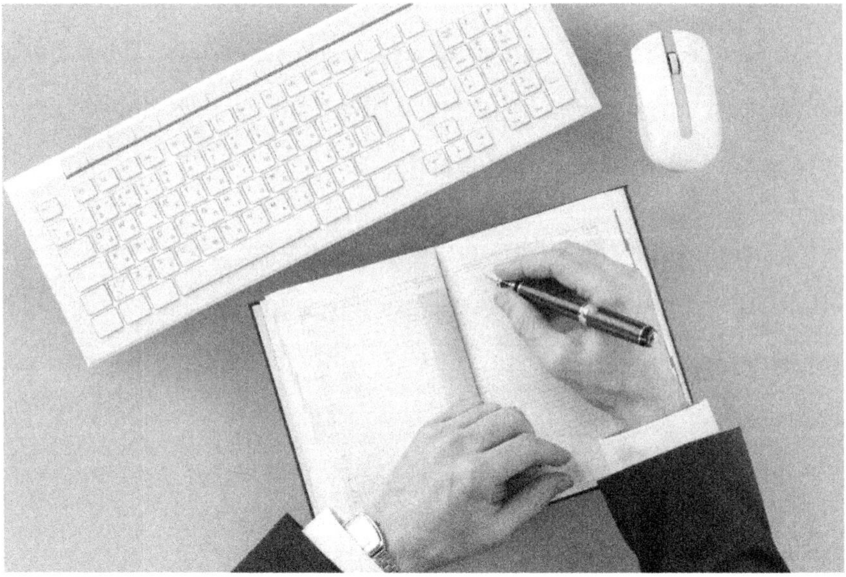

Chapter 2: Defining Your Niche and Value Proposition

In the world of content creation, one of the most crucial decisions you'll make is defining your niche and crafting a compelling value proposition. Your niche is the specific topic or area of focus for your newsletter, while your value proposition is the unique benefit or solution you offer to your target audience. In this chapter, we'll explore the importance of niche selection, guide you through the process of choosing a niche, help you understand your audience, and show you how to create a value proposition that sets your newsletter apart from the competition.

2.1 Importance of Niche Selection

Selecting a niche is a fundamental step in creating a successful Substack newsletter. A well-defined niche not only helps you attract the right audience but also allows you to create targeted, valuable content that resonates with your readers. In this section, we'll delve into the reasons why niche selection is so crucial and explore some examples of successful niches in the newsletter world.

Why Niche Matters

In the crowded landscape of online content, it's essential to stand out from the noise. By focusing on a specific niche, you can differentiate yourself from the competition and establish yourself as an authority in your chosen field. Here are some key reasons why niche selection is so important:

1. Targeted Audience: When you choose a specific niche, you can more easily identify and attract your ideal audience. By creating content that speaks directly to their interests, challenges, and desires, you'll be able to build a loyal and engaged following.

2. Expertise and Credibility: Focusing on a niche allows you to dive deep into a particular topic and develop a high level of expertise. As you consistently create valuable content related to your niche, you'll establish yourself as a credible authority in your field, which can lead to increased trust and loyalty from your audience.

3. Differentiation: In a world where countless newsletters compete for attention, having a clear niche helps you stand out from the crowd. By offering a unique perspective or specialized knowledge in your niche, you'll be able to attract readers who are looking for something specific and valuable.

4. Targeted Marketing: When you know your niche inside and out, it becomes easier to create targeted marketing campaigns that resonate with your ideal audience. You can use niche-specific language, imagery, and channels to reach the people who are most likely to be interested in your content.

5. Potential for Monetization: Having a well-defined niche can open up more opportunities for monetization. When you have a highly targeted audience that trusts your expertise, they may be more willing to pay for premium content, courses, or other products related to your niche.

Examples of Successful Niches

To better understand the power of niche selection, let's take a look at some examples of successful Substack newsletters that have carved out their own unique niches:

1. The Dispatch: Founded by former National Review writers, The Dispatch is a newsletter that focuses on conservative politics and policy analysis. By targeting a specific political niche and offering high-quality, in-depth content, The Dispatch has attracted a loyal following of engaged readers.

2. The Browser: The Browser is a newsletter that curates the best writing and ideas from around the web. By focusing on

a niche of "intellectual curiosity" and carefully selecting thought-provoking articles, The Browser has built a dedicated audience of readers who appreciate its unique perspective and curation.

3. The Hustle: The Hustle is a newsletter that covers business and tech news with a distinctive, conversational tone. By targeting a niche of young, entrepreneurial readers and delivering content in a relatable, engaging way, The Hustle has grown to over 1 million subscribers.

4. The Profile: The Profile is a newsletter that features in-depth interviews and profiles of successful people across various industries. By focusing on a niche of "success stories" and providing valuable insights and inspiration, The Profile has attracted a devoted following of readers who are interested in personal and professional growth.

These examples demonstrate how choosing a specific niche and delivering high-quality, targeted content can lead to success in the newsletter world. By finding your own unique niche and consistently providing value to your audience, you too can build a thriving Substack newsletter.

How to Identify Potential Niches

Now that we've established the importance of niche selection, you might be wondering how to go about identifying potential niches for your own newsletter. Here are some strategies to help you brainstorm and evaluate niche ideas:

1. Reflect on Your Passions and Expertise: Start by considering the topics that you're passionate about and have a deep knowledge of. What subjects do you enjoy learning and talking about? What skills or experiences do you have that others might find valuable?

2. Identify Your Target Audience: Think about the type of people who would be interested in your potential niche. What are their demographics, interests, and challenges? Understanding your target audience can help you evaluate the viability of a niche and tailor your content to their needs.

3. Research the Competition: Look for other newsletters, blogs, or publications that cover your potential niche. Analyze their content, audience, and success to get a sense of the demand and competition in the space. Consider how you could differentiate yourself and provide unique value to readers.

4. Evaluate Market Potential: Assess the potential for growth and monetization in your niche. Are there enough people interested in the topic to build a sizable audience? Are there

opportunities for sponsorships, affiliate marketing, or premium content? A niche with strong market potential will be more sustainable in the long run.

5. Test and Validate: Before fully committing to a niche, test the waters by creating a few pieces of content and sharing them with your target audience. Gauge their response and engagement to see if there's genuine interest in your niche. You can also validate your niche through surveys, interviews, or online communities related to your topic.

By following these strategies and carefully evaluating your options, you'll be well on your way to identifying a strong niche for your Substack newsletter.

Choosing a niche is a critical step in creating a successful Substack newsletter. By focusing on a specific topic or audience, you can differentiate yourself from the competition, establish your expertise, and attract a loyal following of engaged readers. When selecting your niche, consider your passions, target audience, market potential, and opportunities for unique value. By putting in the time and effort to carefully define your niche, you'll lay the foundation for a thriving and sustainable newsletter business.

In the next section, we'll dive deeper into the process of choosing a niche, including how to conduct market research and validate your niche ideas. Stay tuned for more actionable advice and strategies to help you create a successful Substack newsletter.

2.2 How to Choose a Niche

Now that you understand the importance of niche selection, it's time to dive into the process of actually choosing a niche for your Substack newsletter. Selecting the right niche is a crucial decision that will impact the direction and success of your newsletter, so it's essential to approach this process thoughtfully and strategically. In this section, we'll guide you through the steps of identifying your interests and expertise, conducting market research, and validating your niche ideas.

Identifying Your Interests and Expertise

The first step in choosing a niche is to reflect on your own interests, passions, and areas of expertise. Your niche should be something that you genuinely care about and have a deep knowledge of, as this will make it easier to create valuable, engaging content on a consistent basis. Here are some questions to ask yourself when identifying your interests and expertise:

1. What topics do you enjoy learning and talking about? Think about the subjects that you naturally gravitate towards in

your personal and professional life. What do you find yourself reading about, discussing with others, or spending your free time on?

2. What skills or experiences do you have that others might find valuable? Consider your unique background, education, and professional experience. What knowledge or insights have you gained that could be helpful or interesting to others?

3. What problems or challenges have you overcome in your own life? Reflect on the obstacles or difficulties that you've faced and successfully navigated. Your personal experiences and lessons learned could be valuable to readers who are facing similar challenges.

4. What are you known for among your friends, family, or colleagues? Think about the topics or areas where people naturally come to you for advice, guidance, or expertise. These could be potential indicators of your strengths and areas of knowledge.

By answering these questions and reflecting on your own interests and expertise, you'll start to identify potential niches that align with your passions and knowledge base. It's important to choose a niche that you're genuinely excited about, as this will make it easier to stay motivated and committed to creating high-quality content over the long term.

Market Research and Validation

Once you've identified some potential niches based on your interests and expertise, the next step is to conduct market research and validate your ideas. This process involves analyzing the demand, competition, and potential for your niche, to ensure that there's a viable audience and market for your newsletter. Here are some key steps to follow when conducting market research and validation:

1. Analyze the demand for your niche: Start by assessing the overall demand and interest in your potential niche. Use keyword research tools like Google Keyword Planner or SEMrush to see how many people are searching for topics related to your niche. Look for related forums, social media groups, or online communities to gauge the level of engagement and discussion around your niche.

2. Identify your target audience: Develop a clear understanding of who your ideal reader is for your niche. Consider their demographics, interests, challenges, and goals. Creating reader personas can be a helpful way to visualize and understand your target audience.

3. Research the competition: Look for other newsletters, blogs, or publications that cover topics similar to your niche. Analyze their content, audience size, engagement levels, and monetization strategies. Consider how you could differentiate yourself and provide unique value to readers.

4. Evaluate monetization potential: Assess the potential for monetizing your niche through subscriptions, sponsorships, affiliate marketing, or other revenue streams. Look for successful examples of monetization within your niche or related fields.

5. Test and validate your ideas: Before fully committing to a niche, it's important to test and validate your ideas with your target audience. Create a few pieces of sample content related to your niche and share them with potential readers. Gather feedback through surveys, interviews, or online discussions to gauge interest and receptiveness.

By conducting thorough market research and validation, you'll gain valuable insights into the viability and potential of your niche. This process can help you refine your niche, identify opportunities for differentiation, and ensure that there's a real audience and market for your newsletter.

Narrowing Down Your Niche

As you conduct market research and validation, you may find that your initial niche ideas are too broad or competitive. In these cases, it can be helpful to narrow down your niche to a more specific sub-topic or audience. Niche narrowing involves focusing on a more targeted segment of your broader niche, to better differentiate yourself and serve a specific audience. Here are some strategies for narrowing down your niche:

1. Identify sub-topics or sub-niches: Look for more specific topics or sub-niches within your broader niche. For example, if your initial niche is "personal finance," you could narrow it down to "budgeting for millennials" or "investing for retirement."

2. Target a specific audience segment: Consider focusing on a more targeted audience within your niche, based on demographics, interests, or challenges. For example, instead of targeting "entrepreneurs" broadly, you could focus on "female entrepreneurs in the tech industry."

3. Combine multiple interests or areas of expertise: Look for opportunities to combine your various interests or areas of expertise into a unique, intersectional niche. For example, if you're passionate about both travel and sustainability, you

could create a newsletter focused on "eco-friendly travel tips and destinations."

4. Address a specific problem or challenge: Focus your niche on solving a particular problem or challenge that your target audience faces. For example, instead of covering "health and wellness" broadly, you could focus on "overcoming chronic stress and anxiety."

By narrowing down your niche, you can create a more targeted and differentiated newsletter that speaks directly to the needs and interests of your ideal audience. This can help you attract a more engaged and loyal following, and establish yourself as a go-to resource within your specific niche.

Finalizing Your Niche Selection

After conducting market research, validating your ideas, and potentially narrowing down your niche, it's time to make a final decision on your newsletter's focus. Here are some key considerations to keep in mind as you finalize your niche selection:

1. Alignment with your passions and expertise: Ensure that your chosen niche aligns with your genuine interests and areas of knowledge. You'll be creating content on this topic regularly, so it's important to choose something that you're truly passionate about and can speak to with authority.

2. Viability and potential for growth: Consider the long-term viability and growth potential of your niche. Is there a strong and engaged audience for this topic? Are there opportunities for monetization and expansion over time?

3. Differentiation and unique value proposition: Assess how your niche and approach differentiate you from other newsletters or content creators in the space. Ensure that you have a clear and compelling unique value proposition that sets you apart and speaks directly to the needs of your target audience.

4. Scalability and sustainability: Evaluate whether your niche is scalable and sustainable over the long term. Is there enough depth and breadth to the topic to support ongoing content creation? Can you envision yourself consistently creating valuable content on this niche for months or years to come?

By carefully considering these factors and making a thoughtful, strategic decision on your niche, you'll set yourself up for success as you launch and grow your Substack newsletter.

Choosing the right niche is a critical step in creating a successful and sustainable Substack newsletter. By identifying your interests and expertise, conducting market research and validation, narrowing down your focus, and making a strategic final decision, you'll be well-positioned to create a newsletter that resonates with your target audience and stands out in the crowded online landscape.

- Remember, your niche selection is not set in stone – as you grow and evolve your newsletter over time, you may find opportunities to further refine or expand your niche based on audience feedback and market trends. The key is to start with a strong foundation and remain open to adaptation and growth along the way.

In the next section, we'll dive into the process of understanding your target audience on a deeper level, and creating detailed reader personas to guide your content creation and marketing efforts. Stay tuned for more actionable insights and strategies to help you build a thriving newsletter business on Substack.

2.3 Understanding Your Audience

Once you've chosen your niche, the next crucial step is to develop a deep understanding of your target audience. Knowing your audience is essential for creating content that resonates, building a loyal following, and effectively promoting your newsletter. In this section, we'll guide you through the process of defining your target audience, creating detailed reader personas, and using audience insights to inform your content and marketing strategies.

Defining Your Target Audience

Your target audience is the specific group of people who are most likely to be interested in your newsletter and benefit from your content. Defining your target audience involves identifying key characteristics and demographics that unite this group. Here are some factors to consider when defining your target audience:

1. Age: What age range does your ideal reader fall into? Are you targeting a specific generation, such as millennials or baby boomers?

2. Gender: Is your newsletter more likely to appeal to a particular gender, or is it gender-neutral?

3. Location: Are you targeting readers in a specific geographic location, such as a particular country, region, or city?

4. Education level: What is the typical education level of your ideal reader? Are you targeting college graduates, professionals with advanced degrees, or a more general audience?

5. Income level: What is the income range of your target audience? Are you targeting affluent readers, budget-conscious individuals, or somewhere in between?

6. Occupation: Is your newsletter relevant to people in specific industries or job roles? For example, are you targeting entrepreneurs, marketers, or healthcare professionals?

7. Interests and hobbies: What are the common interests, hobbies, or passions of your ideal reader? How do these relate to your newsletter's niche or topic?

8. Challenges and pain points: What are the key challenges, problems, or pain points that your target audience faces? How can your newsletter help address these issues?

By answering these questions and developing a clear picture of your target audience, you'll be better equipped to create content that speaks directly to their needs and interests. Keep in mind that your target audience may evolve over time as your newsletter grows and you gain more insights into your readers.

Creating Reader Personas

While defining your target audience provides a broad overview of your ideal readers, creating detailed reader personas takes this understanding to the next level. A reader persona is a fictional representation of your ideal subscriber, based on real data and insights about your audience. Developing reader personas helps you create more targeted, relevant content and make informed decisions about your newsletter's direction and growth. Here's how to create effective reader personas:

1. Gather data and insights: Start by collecting data and insights about your current subscribers or potential audience. This can include demographic information, survey responses, website analytics, social media insights, and feedback from your readers.

2. Identify common characteristics: Look for patterns and commonalities in the data you've gathered. Group your audience into segments based on shared characteristics, such as age, location, interests, or challenges.

3. Create fictional profiles: For each segment, create a fictional profile that represents your ideal reader. Give each persona a name, age, occupation, and other relevant details. Include a photo or image to make the persona feel more real and relatable.

4. Develop a backstory: Give each persona a backstory that includes their goals, challenges, and motivations. What

drives them to seek out content like yours? What problems are they trying to solve? What are their aspirations and fears?

5. Identify content preferences: Consider each persona's content preferences and consumption habits. What types of content do they enjoy? What formats do they prefer (e.g., long-form articles, short videos, podcasts)? How often do they like to receive content?

6. Refine and update regularly: As you gather more data and insights about your audience, refine and update your reader personas accordingly. Your understanding of your audience should evolve as your newsletter grows and changes.

Here's an example of a reader persona for a newsletter about sustainable living:

Name: Eco-conscious Emma

Age: 32

Location: Portland, Oregon

Occupation: Graphic designer at a small agency

Education: Bachelor's degree in graphic design

Interests: Veganism, zero-waste living, minimalism, yoga

Challenges: Reducing her environmental impact, finding affordable eco-friendly products, balancing sustainability with a busy lifestyle

Goals: To live a more sustainable, intentional life and inspire others to do the same

Content preferences: In-depth articles with practical tips, product recommendations, and inspiring stories of eco-friendly living

By creating detailed reader personas like this, you'll have a clear, actionable understanding of your audience that can guide your content creation, marketing, and growth strategies.

Using Audience Insights to Inform Your Strategy

With your target audience defined and reader personas created, you can start using these insights to inform your newsletter's strategy. Here are some key ways to apply your audience understanding:

1. Tailor your content: Use your reader personas to guide your content creation. What topics, formats, and styles are most likely to resonate with your ideal readers? Create content that directly addresses their interests, challenges, and goals.

2. Optimize your tone and voice: Adjust your writing style and tone to match your audience's preferences. For example, if your target audience is primarily young professionals, you

may want to adopt a more casual, conversational tone than if you were targeting senior executives.

3. Choose relevant promotion channels: Use your audience insights to determine the best channels for promoting your newsletter. Where does your target audience spend their time online? What social media platforms do they use? Focus your promotion efforts on the channels where your ideal readers are most likely to be found.

4. Develop targeted lead magnets: Create lead magnets (such as ebooks, checklists, or templates) that directly address your target audience's challenges and goals. Use these lead magnets to attract new subscribers who fit your ideal reader profile.

5. Segment your email list: As your subscriber base grows, consider segmenting your email list based on your reader personas. This allows you to send more targeted, relevant content to each segment, improving engagement and retention.

6. Inform product and service development: If you plan to offer additional products or services related to your newsletter (such as online courses, coaching, or merchandise), use your audience insights to guide their development. Create

offerings that directly address your ideal readers' needs and desires.

By consistently applying your audience understanding to your newsletter's strategy, you'll be able to create a more targeted, engaging, and valuable experience for your readers, ultimately driving the growth and success of your Substack business.

Understanding your audience is a critical component of building a successful Substack newsletter. By defining your target audience, creating detailed reader personas, and using these insights to inform your content and marketing strategies, you'll be well-positioned to attract and retain a loyal, engaged following.

Remember, understanding your audience is an ongoing process. As your newsletter grows and evolves, continue to gather data and feedback from your readers, and use these insights to refine your personas and strategies over time. The more deeply you understand and serve your audience, the more likely you are to build a thriving, sustainable newsletter business.

In the next section, we'll dive into the process of crafting a compelling value proposition for your newsletter. Your value proposition is the unique promise of value that you make to your target audience, and it's a crucial element of attracting and retaining subscribers. Stay tuned for actionable tips and strategies to help you develop a strong value proposition that sets your newsletter apart in your niche.

2.4 Crafting Your Value Proposition

With a clear understanding of your niche and target audience, the next crucial step is to craft a compelling value proposition for your Substack newsletter. Your value proposition is the unique promise of value that you make to your ideal readers – it's the reason why they should subscribe to your newsletter over others in your niche. In this section, we'll guide you through the process of defining your unique selling points and creating a value proposition that attracts and retains subscribers.

Defining Your Unique Selling Points

Your unique selling points (USPs) are the specific benefits, features, or qualities that set your newsletter apart from the competition. These are the key reasons why your target audience should choose your newsletter over others in your niche. To define your USPs, consider the following questions:

1. What unique expertise or perspective do you bring to your niche? Think about your background, experiences, and

knowledge that give you a distinct viewpoint or authority in your field.

2. What specific problems or challenges do you help your readers solve? Identify the key pain points or goals of your target audience, and consider how your newsletter uniquely addresses these issues.

3. What is your unique style or approach to your content? Do you have a distinctive writing style, tone, or format that sets you apart from other newsletters in your niche?

4. What exclusive content or features do you offer? Consider any special content types, resources, or experiences that are unique to your newsletter, such as interviews with industry experts, downloadable templates, or live Q&A sessions.

5. How does your newsletter deliver value differently than your competitors? Look at other newsletters in your niche and identify the ways in which your newsletter stands out, whether in terms of content depth, frequency, format, or community engagement.

By answering these questions and brainstorming your newsletter's unique qualities, you'll start to develop a list of USPs that you can use to craft your value proposition. Aim to identify 3-5 key USPs that most strongly differentiate your newsletter and resonate with your target audience.

Crafting Your Value Proposition Statement

With your USPs defined, you can now craft a clear, concise value proposition statement that communicates the unique value of your newsletter to potential subscribers. A strong value proposition statement typically includes the following elements:

1. The target audience: Clearly identify who your newsletter is for, using specific descriptors that match your reader personas.

2. The key benefit: State the primary benefit or value that your newsletter provides to your target audience, addressing their main challenge or goal.

3. The unique differentiator: Highlight what sets your newsletter apart from others in your niche, using your key USPs.

Here's a simple template for crafting your value proposition statement:

"For [target audience] who [key challenge or goal], [your newsletter name] provides [key benefit] through [unique differentiator]."

For example, let's say you're creating a newsletter called "Fit and Fabulous Over 50" that provides fitness and wellness advice for women in their 50s and beyond. Your value proposition statement might look like this:

"For women over 50 who want to stay active, healthy, and confident as they age, Fit and Fabulous Over 50 provides practical, science-backed fitness and wellness advice through exclusive interviews with leading experts, personalized workout plans, and a supportive community of like-minded women."

This value proposition statement clearly identifies the target audience (women over 50), the key benefit (staying active, healthy, and confident), and the unique differentiators (exclusive expert interviews, personalized workout plans, and a supportive community).

Refining and Testing Your Value Proposition

Once you've crafted your initial value proposition statement, it's important to refine and test it to ensure it effectively resonates with your target audience. Here are some tips for refining and testing your value proposition:

1. Get feedback from your target audience: Share your value proposition statement with people who fit your ideal reader profile, and ask for their honest feedback. Does the statement

clearly communicate the value of your newsletter? Does it resonate with their needs and interests? Use this feedback to refine your statement.

2. Test different versions: Create a few variations of your value proposition statement, emphasizing different USPs or benefits. Use A/B testing to see which version performs best in terms of attracting subscribers or engaging your audience.

3. Ensure clarity and conciseness: Your value proposition should be easy to understand and communicate. Avoid jargon or overly complex language, and aim to convey your key message in a concise, memorable way.

4. Align with your content: Make sure your value proposition aligns with the actual content and experience you provide in your newsletter. Your newsletter should consistently deliver on the promise of your value proposition.

5. Revisit and update regularly: As your newsletter evolves and your audience grows, revisit your value proposition periodically to ensure it still accurately reflects your unique value and resonates with your readers.

By continually refining and testing your value proposition, you'll be able to create a strong, compelling message that attracts and retains your ideal subscribers.

Communicating Your Value Proposition

With a strong value proposition crafted, it's important to communicate it effectively across all your marketing channels and touchpoints. Here are some key places to showcase your value proposition:

1. Your Substack landing page: Your value proposition should be prominently featured on your Substack landing page, ideally in the header or above-the-fold section. Use clear, compelling copy and visuals to communicate your unique value to potential subscribers.

2. Your newsletter sign up forms: Include a concise version of your value proposition on your newsletter sign-up forms, whether on your website, social media profiles, or other marketing channels. This helps potential subscribers quickly understand the value of subscribing.

3. Your email welcome sequence: When new subscribers sign up for your newsletter, send them a welcome email that reinforces your value proposition and sets expectations for the content and experience they'll receive.

4. Your social media profiles: Use your social media bios and posts to communicate your newsletter's value proposition to your followers. Highlight your USPs and the benefits subscribers can expect.

5. Your content marketing: Infuse your value proposition into your content marketing efforts, such as guest posts, interviews, or social media content. Consistently communicate the unique value of your newsletter to attract new subscribers.

By consistently communicating your value proposition across all your marketing channels, you'll be able to attract and retain subscribers who are the best fit for your newsletter and most likely to engage with and benefit from your content.

Crafting a compelling value proposition is essential for attracting and retaining subscribers for your Substack newsletter. By defining your unique selling points, creating a clear value proposition statement, and effectively communicating your value across your marketing channels, you'll be able to stand out in your niche and build a loyal, engaged audience.

- Remember, your value proposition is not a one-time exercise – it should be a living, evolving part of your newsletter strategy. Continuously refine and test your value proposition based on subscriber feedback and market trends, and ensure that your newsletter consistently delivers on the unique value you promise.

With a strong value proposition as the foundation, you're ready to move on to the next crucial aspect of your newsletter strategy: crafting engaging, valuable content that keeps your subscribers coming back for more. In the next chapter, we'll dive into the key principles and tactics of creating compelling newsletter content, from developing your content strategy to writing irresistible headlines and crafting engaging stories. Stay tuned for more actionable insights and tips to help you create a newsletter that truly stands out in your niche.

Chapter 3: Crafting Engaging Content

Creating compelling, valuable content is the heart of your Substack newsletter's success. Your content is what attracts and retains subscribers, establishes your authority in your niche, and ultimately drives the growth of your newsletter business. In this chapter, we'll dive into the key principles and tactics of crafting engaging newsletter content, from developing your content strategy to writing irresistible headlines and crafting compelling stories that keep your readers coming back for more.

3.1 Content Strategy Basics

Before you start creating content for your Substack newsletter, it's essential to develop a clear, purposeful content strategy. Your content strategy is the foundation that guides your content creation efforts, ensuring that your newsletter consistently delivers value to your target audience and supports your business goals. In this section, we'll explore the key components of a strong content strategy and provide actionable tips for developing your own strategy.

Defining Your Content Goals and Objectives

The first step in developing your content strategy is to define your content goals and objectives. What do you want to achieve with your newsletter content? Your goals should be specific, measurable, achievable, relevant, and time-bound (SMART). Some common content goals for Substack newsletters include:

1. Growing your subscriber base: Creating content that attracts new subscribers and encourages existing readers to share your newsletter with others.

2. Establishing your authority and expertise: Crafting content that showcases your unique knowledge, insights, and perspectives in your niche, positioning you as a trusted expert.

3. Engaging and retaining subscribers: Developing content that resonates with your target audience, sparks conversations, and keeps readers eagerly anticipating your next newsletter.

4. Driving revenue: Creating content that promotes your paid subscription offerings, affiliate products, or sponsored content opportunities.

When defining your content goals, consider how they align with your overall business objectives and your unique value proposition.

Your content should consistently reinforce your brand identity and the unique benefits you offer to your target audience.

Understanding Your Audience's Content Needs and Preferences

To create content that truly resonates with your readers, you need to have a deep understanding of your audience's needs, preferences, and behaviors. Use the audience insights and reader personas you developed in Chapter 2 to inform your content strategy. Consider questions such as:

1. What topics and subtopics are most relevant and valuable to your target audience? Look for the key challenges, goals, and interests that drive your ideal readers.

2. What content formats does your audience prefer? Do they enjoy long-form articles, short and snappy tips, visual content, or a mix of formats?

3. What tone and style resonate with your readers? Should your content be informative and educational, entertaining and humorous, or inspirational and thought-provoking?

4. What content channels does your audience use? Where do they typically consume content related to your niche, such as social media platforms, blogs, or industry publications?

By understanding your audience's content needs and preferences, you can create a content strategy that delivers the right content, in the right format, through the right channels, to the right people.

Conducting a Content Audit and Gap Analysis

Before you start creating new content for your newsletter, it's helpful to conduct a content audit and gap analysis. A content audit involves reviewing and evaluating your existing content, if any, to assess its performance, relevance, and alignment with your current goals and audience needs. A gap analysis helps you identify areas where you're missing content that your audience wants or needs.

To conduct a content audit, follow these steps:

1. Inventory your existing content: Create a spreadsheet or document listing all your existing newsletter content, including the title, topic, format, publication date, and any relevant metrics (e.g., open rates, click-through rates, shares).

2. Evaluate each piece of content: Review each newsletter issue or article and assess its quality, relevance, and performance. Look for patterns in the types of content that perform well or poorly with your audience.

3. Identify content gaps: Look for topics, subtopics, or content formats that are missing from your existing content but are

relevant and valuable to your target audience. Consider using keyword research tools, social media listening, or audience surveys to uncover content gaps.

4. Prioritize content opportunities: Based on your content audit and gap analysis, identify the most promising opportunities for new content creation or optimization. Prioritize content ideas that align with your goals, audience needs, and resources.

By regularly conducting content audits and gap analyses, you can ensure that your content strategy remains relevant, effective, and aligned with your evolving business goals and audience needs.

Developing Your Content Pillars and Themes

With your content goals, audience insights, and content gaps in mind, the next step is to develop your content pillars and themes. Content pillars are the core topics or categories that your newsletter content will focus on, while themes are the specific angles, perspectives, or approaches you'll take within each pillar.

To develop your content pillars, consider the following tips:

1. Align with your niche and value proposition: Your content pillars should be directly related to your newsletter's niche and the unique value you offer to your target audience.

2. Cover the full breadth of your niche: Aim to create content pillars that comprehensively address the key aspects, challenges, and opportunities within your niche.

3. Balance breadth and depth: While you want to cover a range of topics within your niche, also ensure that each pillar is focused enough to allow for deep, substantive exploration.

4. Consider your audience's journey: Develop content pillars that address your audience's needs and interests at different stages of their journey, from awareness to consideration to decision-making.

Once you've identified your core content pillars, brainstorm specific themes and angles you can explore within each pillar. For example, if one of your content pillars is "Productivity Tips for Entrepreneurs," your themes might include:

Time management strategies

Goal-setting and prioritization techniques

Overcoming procrastination and distractions

Productivity tools and technology

Work-life balance and self-care

By developing a mix of evergreen and timely themes within each pillar, you can create a content strategy that is both comprehensive and adaptable to changing audience needs and interests.

Creating a Content Calendar and Publishing Schedule

With your content pillars and themes defined, the final step in developing your content strategy is to create a content calendar and publishing schedule. A content calendar is a planning tool that outlines the specific topics, formats, and publication dates for your upcoming newsletter content. A publishing schedule defines the frequency and timing of your newsletter issues.

To create your content calendar, follow these steps:

1. Determine your publishing frequency: Decide how often you'll publish your newsletter, whether it's weekly, bi-weekly, monthly, or another interval. Consider your audience's preferences, your content production capacity, and your overall goals.

2. Map out your content themes and formats: Using your content pillars and themes as a guide, brainstorm specific newsletter topics and formats for the coming weeks or months. Consider a mix of evergreen and timely content, as

well as different formats like long-form articles, short tips, interviews, or roundups.

3. Schedule your content: Plot out your newsletter topics and formats on a calendar, assigning each piece of content a specific publication date. Consider factors like seasonality, current events, and any promotions or launches you have planned.

4. Build in flexibility: While it's important to have a content plan, also allow for some flexibility to adapt to changing circumstances or new opportunities. Build in some buffer time or "wildcard" slots in your calendar for timely or spontaneous content.

5. Use a content planning tool: Consider using a content planning tool like Trello, Asana, or CoSchedule to create and manage your content calendar. These tools can help you visualize your content plan, collaborate with team members, and keep your production workflow organized.

By creating a clear, purposeful content calendar and publishing schedule, you can ensure a consistent flow of valuable content for your subscribers while also streamlining your content production process.

Developing a strong content strategy is essential for the success of your Substack newsletter. By defining your content goals, understanding your audience's needs, conducting a content audit and gap analysis, developing your content pillars and themes, and creating a content calendar and publishing schedule, you'll have a solid foundation for crafting engaging, valuable content that resonates with your readers and supports your business objectives.

- Remember, your content strategy is not a one-time exercise, but an ongoing process of planning, creation, evaluation, and optimization. As you publish and promote your newsletter content, continually monitor your performance metrics, gather reader feedback, and adapt your strategy based on what's working and what's not.

With a clear, purposeful content strategy guiding your efforts, you're well on your way to creating a newsletter that truly stands out in your niche and delivers exceptional value to your subscribers. In the next section, we'll dive into the specifics of creating an editorial calendar and managing your content production workflow. Stay tuned for more actionable tips and best practices to help you streamline your content creation process and deliver high-quality newsletter content consistently.

3.2 Editorial Calendar

An editorial calendar is a crucial tool for managing your content strategy and ensuring a consistent, high-quality flow of newsletter content. It helps you plan, organize, and schedule your content in advance, allowing you to streamline your production process and maintain a steady publishing cadence. In this section, we'll explore the importance of editorial calendars and provide actionable tips for creating and managing your own calendar.

Why You Need an Editorial Calendar

An editorial calendar offers numerous benefits for your Substack newsletter, including:

1. Consistency: An editorial calendar helps you maintain a consistent publishing schedule, which is essential for building reader trust and engagement. By planning your content in advance, you can ensure that you always have fresh, relevant content ready to go, even during busy or challenging times.

2. Organization: With an editorial calendar, you can keep track of all your content ideas, assignments, and deadlines in one centralized place. This helps you stay organized and avoid last-minute scrambles or content gaps.

3. Strategic planning: An editorial calendar allows you to take a strategic, big-picture view of your content. You can plan your content around key dates, events, or promotions, and ensure that your newsletter aligns with your overall business goals and objectives.

4. Collaboration: If you work with a team or collaborate with guest contributors, an editorial calendar is essential for keeping everyone on the same page. It allows you to assign tasks, set deadlines, and track progress in a transparent, accessible way.

5. Flexibility: While an editorial calendar provides structure and planning, it also allows for flexibility. You can easily adjust your content plan as needed based on new ideas, changing circumstances, or reader feedback.

By incorporating an editorial calendar into your content workflow, you can streamline your production process, improve your content quality and consistency, and ultimately drive better results for your Substack newsletter.

Creating Your Editorial Calendar

Now that you understand the importance of an editorial calendar, let's walk through the steps of creating your own:

1. Choose your planning timeframe: Decide on the timeframe for your editorial calendar, whether it's weekly, monthly, quarterly, or another interval. Consider your publishing frequency, content production capacity, and overall goals when choosing your timeframe.

2. Identify key dates and events: Look ahead at the coming months and identify any key dates, events, or milestones that you want to plan content around. This could include holidays, industry events, product launches, or special promotions.

3. Brainstorm content ideas: Using your content pillars and themes as a guide, brainstorm a list of specific content ideas for your upcoming newsletters. Consider a mix of evergreen and timely topics, as well as different formats like articles, interviews, roundups, or multimedia content.

4. Prioritize and assign content: Review your content ideas and prioritize the ones that align best with your goals, audience needs, and resources. Assign each piece of content to a specific newsletter issue or publication date.

5. Determine production tasks and deadlines: Break down each piece of content into its component production tasks, such as research, writing, editing, and design. Assign deadlines for each task to ensure a smooth, timely production process.

6. Choose your calendar format: Decide on the format for your editorial calendar, whether it's a spreadsheet, a project management tool, or a specialized content calendar software. Choose a format that is easy to use, visually appealing, and accessible to all relevant team members.

7. Input your content and deadlines: Input your planned content, tasks, and deadlines into your chosen calendar format. Be sure to include all relevant details, such as the content title, author, format, and publication date.

8. Review and adjust regularly: Review your editorial calendar regularly to ensure that it remains up-to-date and aligned with your goals. Make adjustments as needed based on new ideas, changing priorities, or performance data.

By following these steps, you can create a clear, comprehensive editorial calendar that helps you plan, organize, and execute your content strategy with greater efficiency and effectiveness.

Best Practices for Managing Your Editorial Calendar

Once you've created your editorial calendar, it's important to establish some best practices for managing it effectively. Here are some tips to keep in mind:

1. Set realistic deadlines: When assigning deadlines for your content tasks, be realistic about the time and resources required. Build in some buffer time to account for unexpected delays or revisions.

2. Communicate clearly: If you're working with a team or external contributors, make sure to communicate your editorial calendar and expectations clearly. Provide detailed briefs, guidelines, and feedback to ensure that everyone is aligned and producing high-quality work.

3. Use visual cues: Use color-coding, tags, or other visual cues to help you quickly identify different types of content, stages of production, or priority levels within your calendar.

4. Build in flexibility: While it's important to have a plan, also allow for some flexibility in your calendar. Build in some "wildcard" slots or buffer time to accommodate new ideas, timely topics, or reader requests.

5. Monitor and measure: Regularly monitor your content performance and gather reader feedback to assess the effectiveness of your editorial calendar. Use this data to inform future content planning and optimization.

6. Celebrate successes: As you execute your editorial calendar and publish high-quality content, take time to celebrate your successes and recognize the hard work of your team. This can help keep everyone motivated and engaged in the content creation process.

By establishing these best practices and consistently managing your editorial calendar, you can ensure a smooth, efficient content production process that delivers value to your readers and supports your business goals.

Tools for Managing Your Editorial Calendar

There are many tools available to help you create, manage, and collaborate on your editorial calendar. Here are some popular options to consider:

1. Google Sheets: Google Sheets is a simple, accessible option for creating and sharing your editorial calendar. You can use a spreadsheet template or create your own custom format, and easily collaborate with team members in real-time.

2. Trello: Trello is a visual project management tool that uses boards, lists, and cards to help you organize and track your content production. You can create a board for your editorial calendar, with lists for each stage of production and cards for each piece of content.

3. Asana: Asana is another popular project management tool that allows you to create tasks, assign deadlines, and track progress for your content production. You can create a project for your editorial calendar and use tags, comments, and attachments to keep everything organized.

4. CoSchedule: CoSchedule is a specialized content marketing calendar that integrates with your WordPress site, social media accounts, and other tools. It allows you to plan, schedule, and promote your content all in one place.

5. Airtable: Airtable is a flexible, database-style platform that allows you to create custom content calendars with various views, fields, and filters. It's a good option if you have a complex content operation with multiple contributors, channels, or formats.

Ultimately, the best tool for your editorial calendar will depend on your specific needs, preferences, and budget. Choose a tool that is easy to use, visually appealing, and allows for seamless collaboration and communication with your team.

An editorial calendar is a powerful tool for organizing, planning, and executing your content strategy for your Substack newsletter. By creating a comprehensive calendar that aligns with your goals, audience needs, and resources, you can ensure a consistent flow of high-quality content that engages your readers and drives your business forward.

- Remember to choose a calendar format and tool that works for you, and establish clear best practices for managing your calendar effectively. Regularly review and adjust your calendar based on performance data and reader feedback, and celebrate your successes along the way.

With a well-managed editorial calendar as the backbone of your content operation, you'll be well-equipped to create compelling, valuable content that sets your Substack newsletter apart and keeps your readers coming back for more.

In the next section, we'll explore the various types of content you can create for your newsletter, from articles and podcasts to videos and more. We'll provide tips and best practices for crafting engaging, multimedia content that resonates with your audience and supports your business objectives. Stay tuned for more actionable insights and strategies to help you take your newsletter content to the next level.

3.3 Types of Content

One of the key advantages of Substack is the flexibility it offers in terms of content formats. As a newsletter creator, you have the freedom to experiment with various types of content to engage your audience and deliver value in unique ways. In this section, we'll explore some of the most popular content formats for Substack newsletters, along with tips and best practices for creating each type of content effectively.

Articles

Articles are the most common type of content found in Substack newsletters. They are written pieces that provide information, insights, or opinions on a particular topic. Articles can range from short, snappy blog posts to long-form, in-depth essays, depending on your niche and audience preferences.

When creating articles for your newsletter, consider the following tips:

1. Choose relevant, engaging topics: Select article topics that align with your niche and resonate with your target audience. Use your content pillars and themes as a guide, and consider timely or trending topics that will capture your readers' attention.

2. Craft compelling headlines: Your article headline is the first thing readers will see, so it's essential to make it engaging

and clickable. Use strong, active language and clearly communicate the value or benefit of reading the article.

3. Structure your content effectively: Use subheadings, bullet points, and short paragraphs to break up your content and make it easier to read. Follow a logical structure that guides readers through your main points and supports your central argument or theme.

4. Provide valuable insights and takeaways: Ensure that your articles offer genuine value to your readers, whether it's practical advice, thought-provoking ideas, or unique perspectives. Include clear takeaways or action steps that readers can apply to their own lives or work.

5. Incorporate storytelling and examples: Use storytelling techniques and real-life examples to make your articles more engaging and relatable. Share personal anecdotes, case studies, or hypothetical scenarios to illustrate your points and connect with your readers on a deeper level.

6. Edit and proofread carefully: Before publishing your articles, take the time to edit and proofread them thoroughly. Check for grammar and spelling errors, ensure that your ideas flow logically, and cut any unnecessary or repetitive content.

By following these tips and consistently creating high-quality, valuable articles, you can establish your newsletter as a go-to resource in your niche and keep your readers coming back for more.

Podcasts

Podcasts are audio content that can be a great way to add variety and depth to your Substack newsletter. By incorporating podcast episodes into your content mix, you can provide your subscribers with a more immersive, intimate experience and cater to those who prefer to consume content on the go.

Here are some tips for creating effective podcast content for your newsletter:

1. Determine your podcast format: Decide on the format that best suits your niche and audience. Common podcast formats include interviews, solo commentary, panel discussions, and storytelling or narrative-style episodes.

2. Invest in quality audio equipment: To create professional-sounding podcast episodes, invest in a good-quality microphone, recording software, and editing tools. Ensure that your audio is clear, crisp, and free of background noise or distortions.

3. Plan and script your episodes: While you don't need to script your entire podcast word-for-word, it's important to have a clear outline and structure for each episode. Plan your main points, questions, and transitions in advance to ensure a smooth, coherent flow.

4. Choose engaging, knowledgeable guests: If you're doing an interview-style podcast, choose guests who are engaging, knowledgeable, and relevant to your niche. Look for guests who can provide unique insights, experiences, or perspectives that will be valuable to your listeners.

5. Promote your podcast episodes: When you publish a new podcast episode, promote it across your other marketing channels, such as social media, your website, or your email list. Use engaging visuals, quotes, or teasers to entice people to listen.

6. Encourage listener engagement: Encourage your listeners to engage with your podcast by asking for feedback, questions, or topic suggestions. You can also create a dedicated discussion thread or community space for listeners to connect and discuss each episode.

By incorporating podcast episodes into your Substack newsletter, you can provide your subscribers with a more dynamic, engaging content experience and build a deeper, more personal connection with your audience.

Videos

Videos are another powerful content format that can help you stand out in your subscribers' inboxes and deliver value in a more visual, engaging way. Whether you create short, snappy video tutorials or longer, in-depth video essays, incorporating video content into your newsletter can be a great way to mix up your content and cater to different learning styles.

Here are some tips for creating effective video content for your Substack newsletter:

1. Choose your video style and format: Determine the video style and format that best aligns with your niche and audience preferences. Common video formats for newsletters include tutorials, interviews, product reviews, or behind-the-scenes glimpses into your work or life.

2. Invest in quality video equipment: To create professional-looking videos, invest in a good-quality camera, microphone, and lighting equipment. Ensure that your videos are well-lit, in focus, and have clear, crisp audio.

3. Plan and script your videos: Like with podcasts, it's important to have a clear plan and structure for your videos. Create an outline or script that covers your main points, demonstrations, or interview questions, and practice your delivery to ensure a smooth, engaging flow.

4. Keep your videos concise and focused: While longer videos can work well for certain topics or formats, aim to keep most of your newsletter videos concise and focused. Aim for a length of 5-10 minutes for most videos, and ensure that each video has a clear, specific purpose or takeaway.

5. Optimize your videos for email: When embedding videos in your newsletter, ensure that they are optimized for email clients and mobile devices. Use a reliable video hosting platform, such as YouTube or Vimeo, and include a clear thumbnail image and play button to entice clicks.

6. Promote your videos across channels: As with podcasts, promote your newsletter videos across your other marketing channels to drive views and engagement. Share teaser clips or behind-the-scenes snippets on social media, and encourage your subscribers to share your videos with their own networks.

By incorporating video content into your Substack newsletter, you can create a more dynamic, engaging content experience for your subscribers and showcase your expertise or personality in a more visual, memorable way.

Other Content Formats

In addition to articles, podcasts, and videos, there are many other content formats you can experiment with in your Substack newsletter. Here are a few ideas to consider:

1. Infographics: Infographics are visual representations of information or data that can be a great way to make complex topics more accessible and shareable. Use tools like Canva or Venngage to create eye-catching infographics that complement your written content.

2. Quizzes and polls: Interactive content like quizzes and polls can be a fun way to engage your subscribers and gather insights into their preferences or knowledge. Use tools like Typeform or SurveyMonkey to create quizzes or polls that relate to your niche or content themes.

3. Downloadable resources: Offer your subscribers downloadable resources like ebooks, checklists, or templates that provide additional value and help them apply your insights to their own lives or work. Use tools like Canva or

Adobe InDesign to create professional-looking downloadable resources.

4. Curated content roundups: Create roundup posts that curate the best content or resources related to your niche from around the web. This can be a great way to provide additional value to your subscribers while also building relationships with other creators or brands in your space.

5. Guest posts or collaborations: Collaborate with other creators or experts in your niche to create guest posts, interviews, or joint projects for your newsletter. This can be a great way to bring fresh perspectives and cross-promote your newsletter to new audiences.

By experimenting with different content formats and finding the right mix for your audience, you can create a more varied, engaging newsletter experience that keeps your subscribers coming back for more.

Creating engaging, valuable content is at the heart of building a successful Substack newsletter. By experimenting with different content formats like articles, podcasts, videos, and more, you can cater to different learning styles and preferences and keep your subscribers engaged and excited about your newsletter.

- Remember to always prioritize quality and value in your content creation, and to continuously gather feedback and insights from your audience to refine your content strategy over time. With a commitment to creating exceptional content and a willingness to experiment and adapt, you can build a loyal, engaged subscriber base that looks forward to every new issue of your newsletter.

In the next section, we'll dive into the specifics of writing for your newsletter, including tips and best practices for crafting engaging headlines, structuring your content effectively, and using multimedia elements to enhance your writing. Stay tuned for more actionable insights and strategies to help you take your newsletter writing to the next level.

3.4 Writing Tips and Best Practices

Now that you understand the different types of content you can create for your Substack newsletter, it's time to dive into the specifics of writing compelling, engaging content that resonates with your audience. In this section, we'll explore some key tips and best practices for crafting irresistible headlines, structuring your content effectively, and using multimedia elements to enhance your writing.

Writing Engaging Headlines

Your headline is the first thing readers will see when your newsletter lands in their inbox, so it's essential to make it as compelling and clickable as possible. A great headline can be the difference between a subscriber opening your newsletter or sending it straight to the trash. Here are some tips for writing engaging headlines:

1. Keep it clear and concise: Your headline should clearly communicate the main topic or benefit of your content in a concise, easy-to-understand way. Aim for headlines that are around 6-12 words long, and avoid using complex jargon or obscure references.

2. Use strong, active language: Use powerful, active verbs and strong, emotional language to make your headlines more impactful and engaging. Words like "discover," "unleash," "transform," and "revolutionize" can help create a sense of excitement and urgency.

3. Highlight the benefit or value: Focus your headline on the key benefit or value that your content provides to the reader. Use words like "how to," "why," or "secrets" to communicate the practical, actionable insights readers will gain from your content.

4. Incorporate numbers and lists: Headlines that incorporate numbers or lists (e.g., "10 Ways to Boost Your Productivity" or "The Top 5 Trends in Your Industry") can be particularly effective at grabbing readers' attention and promising a clear, scannable structure.

5. Test and optimize: Don't be afraid to experiment with different headline variations and test their performance over time. Use your newsletter analytics to track which headlines generate the highest open and click-through rates, and use those insights to continually refine your approach.

By crafting clear, compelling headlines that highlight the value and benefit of your content, you can dramatically increase the chances of your subscribers opening and engaging with your newsletter.

Structuring Your Content

Once you've captured your readers' attention with a great headline, it's important to structure your content in a way that keeps them engaged and makes your key points easy to follow and absorb. Here are some tips for structuring your newsletter content effectively:

1. Start with a strong introduction: Your introduction should hook readers' attention and clearly communicate what they can expect to learn or gain from your content. Use

storytelling, questions, or bold statements to create a sense of intrigue and motivate readers to keep reading.

2. Use subheadings to break up your content: Subheadings are a great way to break your content into clear, scannable sections and help readers navigate your key points. Use descriptive, keyword-rich subheadings that communicate the main topic or takeaway of each section.

3. Keep paragraphs short and focused: Long, dense paragraphs can be intimidating and difficult to read, especially on mobile devices. Aim for paragraphs that are 2-4 sentences long, and focus each paragraph on a single main idea or point.

4. Use bullet points and numbered lists: Bullet points and numbered lists are a great way to break up your content and make key information easy to scan and absorb. Use them to highlight important takeaways, steps in a process, or examples that support your main points.

5. Incorporate transitions and signposts: Use transitional phrases and signposts to guide readers through your content and help them follow your argument or narrative. Phrases like "however," "in addition," or "as a result" can help create a sense of logical flow and progression.

6. End with a strong conclusion and call-to-action: Your conclusion should reinforce your main points and leave readers with a clear sense of what they've learned or gained from your content. End with a strong call-to-action that encourages readers to take a specific next step, such as leaving a comment, sharing your newsletter, or checking out a related resource.

By structuring your content in a clear, logical way that emphasizes your key points and makes your writing easy to follow and engage with, you can keep readers hooked from start to finish and increase the impact and memorability of your newsletter.

Using Multimedia Elements

In addition to text, incorporating multimedia elements like images, videos, and audio clips can be a powerful way to enhance your newsletter content and make it more engaging and memorable. Here are some tips for using multimedia elements effectively:

1. Choose high-quality, relevant visuals: When selecting images or videos to include in your newsletter, choose high-quality, visually appealing assets that are directly relevant to your content. Avoid generic stock photos or low-resolution images that can make your newsletter look unprofessional.

2. Use images to break up text and add visual interest: Placing images throughout your newsletter can help break up long blocks of text and add visual interest that keeps readers engaged. Aim to include an image every 300-500 words, and use descriptive captions to provide context and reinforce your key points.

3. Embed videos and audio clips: If you've created video or audio content that complements your newsletter topic, consider embedding it directly in your newsletter using a service like YouTube or Vimeo. This can be a great way to provide additional value to your subscribers and showcase your multimedia content.

4. Optimize images and videos for email: When including images or videos in your newsletter, be sure to optimize them for email delivery and mobile viewing. Use compressed image files to reduce load times, and include descriptive alt text for subscribers who may have images disabled.

5. Use infographics and data visualizations: If your newsletter content includes data or statistics, consider using infographics or data visualizations to make that information more engaging and easy to understand. Tools like Canva or

Venngage make it easy to create professional-looking infographics without any design experience.

6. Experiment with GIFs and animations: Used sparingly, GIFs and animations can be a fun way to add some personality and humor to your newsletter content. Just be sure to use them in a way that complements your brand voice and doesn't distract from your main message.

By incorporating relevant, high-quality multimedia elements into your newsletter content, you can create a more engaging, visually appealing experience for your subscribers that reinforces your key points and helps your content stand out in a crowded inbox.

Conclusion

Writing compelling, engaging content is essential for building a loyal, enthusiastic audience for your Substack newsletter. By crafting irresistible headlines, structuring your content for maximum impact, and incorporating relevant multimedia elements, you can create a newsletter experience that keeps subscribers coming back for more.

- Remember, writing great newsletter content is a skill that develops over time, so don't be afraid to experiment with different approaches and continually refine your technique based on subscriber feedback and analytics. Stay focused on providing genuine value and insight to your readers, and always strive to make your writing as clear, concise, and engaging as possible.

In the next chapter, we'll explore the key principles of designing a professional, visually appealing newsletter that reflects your unique brand and style. From choosing the right template to incorporating eye-catching visuals and ensuring mobile responsiveness, you'll learn everything you need to know to create a newsletter that looks as great as the content inside it. Stay tuned for more tips and best practices to help you take your newsletter to the next level!

Chapter 4: Designing Your Newsletter

The design of your Substack newsletter plays a crucial role in engaging your readers and creating a professional, memorable brand. A well-designed newsletter not only enhances the reading experience but also reinforces your unique style and personality. In this chapter, we'll explore the key principles of effective newsletter design, from selecting the perfect template to customizing your header, optimizing typography, and incorporating visuals that captivate your audience.

4.1 Selecting a Template

Choosing the right template for your Substack newsletter is the first step in creating a visually appealing and functional design. Substack offers a range of pre-designed templates that cater to various styles and preferences, making it easy to find one that aligns with your brand and content. In this section, we'll guide you through the process of selecting the perfect template and customizing it to make it truly your own.

Understanding the Importance of a Good Template

Your newsletter template is the foundation of your design, setting the tone and structure for your content. A well-chosen template can:

1. **Enhance readability:** A good template organizes your content in a clear, logical manner, making it easy for readers to navigate and consume your newsletter.

2. **Reflect your brand identity:** Your template should align with your brand's visual style, colors, and personality, creating a consistent and recognizable experience for your subscribers.

3. **Improve engagement:** An attractive, professional-looking template can capture readers' attention and encourage them to spend more time exploring your content.

4. **Simplify your workflow:** By starting with a pre-designed template, you can save time and effort on the design process, allowing you to focus on creating great content.

When selecting a template, it's essential to consider your specific content needs, target audience, and brand identity to ensure that your choice effectively supports your goals.

Exploring Substack's Template Options

Substack offers a curated selection of newsletter templates designed to suit a variety of niches, styles, and purposes. To browse the available templates:

1. Log in to your Substack account and navigate to your publication's "Settings" page.

2. Click on the "Design" tab in the left sidebar.

3. In the "Template" section, click on the "Change Template" button.

4. Browse through the available templates, previewing how each one would look with your content.

Take your time exploring the different templates, considering factors such as:

Layout: How is the content organized? Does the template have a single-column or multi-column layout? How are images and other media incorporated?

Typography: What fonts are used for headlines, subheadings, and body text? Are they easy to read and visually appealing?

Color scheme: Does the template use a color palette that complements your brand? Is there sufficient contrast between text and background colors?

Branding elements: Does the template provide space for your logo, tagline, or other branding elements?

Responsive design: How does the template look on different devices, such as desktop computers, tablets, and smartphones? Is the design optimized for mobile reading?

By carefully evaluating each template option against your specific needs and preferences, you'll be better equipped to select one that effectively showcases your content and engages your audience.

Customizing Your Chosen Template

Once you've selected a template that aligns with your vision, Substack allows you to customize various aspects of the design to make it uniquely yours. Some key elements you can customize include:

1. **Colors:** Modify the color scheme to match your brand palette, ensuring a cohesive and professional look.

2. **Fonts:** Choose typography that reflects your brand personality and enhances readability. Substack offers a range of font options, or you can upload your own custom fonts.

3. **Logo and branding:** Upload your logo and other branding elements, such as a favicon or social media icons, to reinforce your brand identity throughout your newsletter.

4. **Header and footer:** Customize the content and layout of your newsletter's header and footer, including elements like your publication name, tagline, navigation links, and contact information.

5. **Background and borders:** Adjust the background color or image, as well as the style and color of borders and dividers, to create visual interest and separation between sections.

To access these customization options, navigate to the "Design" tab in your Substack settings and explore the various settings under "Styles," "Header," "Footer," and other relevant sections. Experiment with different combinations of colors, fonts, and layouts until you achieve a design that feels authentic to your brand and engaging for your readers.

Best Practices for Template Customization

As you customize your chosen template, keep the following best practices in mind:

1. **Prioritize readability:** Above all, your newsletter design should prioritize readability. Ensure that your font choices,

colors, and layout make your content easy and enjoyable to read.

2. **Maintain consistency:** Use consistent branding elements, colors, and styles throughout your newsletter to create a cohesive and professional appearance.

3. **Simplify your design:** Avoid overcrowding your template with too many colors, fonts, or design elements. A clean, simple design is often more effective at engaging readers and communicating your message.

4. **Optimize for different devices:** Test your customized template on various devices and email clients to ensure that it looks and functions as intended across different screens and platforms.

5. **Gather feedback:** Share your customized template with trusted friends, colleagues, or a sample of your target audience to gather feedback and suggestions for improvement.

By selecting a template that aligns with your brand and content goals, and customizing it to make it distinctly yours, you'll create a strong visual foundation for your Substack newsletter that engages and delights your readers.

4.2 Customizing Your Header

Your newsletter header is one of the first things your subscribers will see when they open your email, making it a crucial element of your design. A well-designed header not only captures your readers' attention but also reinforces your brand identity and sets the tone for your content. In this section, we'll explore the key considerations for designing a compelling header and guide you through the process of customizing your header in Substack.

The Importance of a Strong Header

Your newsletter header serves several important functions:

1. **Branding:** Your header is a prime opportunity to showcase your logo, colors, and other visual elements that represent your brand. A consistent, recognizable header helps build brand awareness and loyalty among your subscribers.

2. **Navigation:** Your header can include navigation links to key sections of your newsletter or website, making it easy for readers to find the content they're interested in.

3. **Setting expectations:** The design and content of your header can communicate the tone, style, and purpose of your newsletter, helping set expectations for your readers.

4. **Encouraging engagement:** An eye-catching, visually appealing header can grab readers' attention and encourage them to engage with your content.

When designing your header, consider how you can use visual elements, layout, and content to achieve these goals and create a strong first impression with your subscribers.

Key Elements of a Compelling Header

A compelling newsletter header typically includes several key elements:

1. **Logo:** Your logo is the cornerstone of your brand identity. Place your logo prominently in your header to reinforce your brand and make your newsletter instantly recognizable.

2. **Publication name:** Include your publication name in your header, either as part of your logo or as separate text. This helps remind subscribers what newsletter they're reading and can be especially useful if your subject line doesn't include your publication name.

3. **Tagline or value proposition:** Consider including a short tagline or value proposition in your header that communicates the key benefit or purpose of your newsletter.

This can help reinforce your brand messaging and encourage subscribers to engage with your content.

4. **Navigation links:** If your newsletter includes multiple sections or regular features, consider adding navigation links to your header. This can make it easier for subscribers to find the content they're most interested in and encourage deeper engagement with your newsletter.

5. **Visual elements:** Use colors, shapes, and other visual elements to make your header eye-catching and visually appealing. Consider how you can use these elements to reinforce your brand identity and create a cohesive visual experience for your subscribers.

When designing your header, aim for a balance of clarity, visual appeal, and brand consistency. Keep your header simple and uncluttered, with a clear hierarchy of information and a focus on the most important elements.

Customizing Your Header in Substack

Substack provides a range of customization options for your newsletter header, allowing you to create a unique and professional design that aligns with your brand. To access these options:

1. Log in to your Substack account and navigate to your publication's "Settings" page.

2. Click on the "Design" tab in the left sidebar.

3. Scroll down to the "Header" section.

From here, you can customize various aspects of your header, including:

1. **Logo:** Upload your logo image in PNG, JPG, or GIF format. Substack recommends using a logo with a maximum width of 600 pixels and a height of 150-200 pixels for optimal display across devices.

2. **Publication name and tagline:** Enter your publication name and tagline in the provided fields. You can customize the font, size, color, and alignment of these elements using the styling options below.

3. **Navigation links:** Add navigation links to key sections of your newsletter or website. You can customize the text, URL, and style of each link.

4. **Background color or image:** Choose a background color or upload a background image for your header. If using an

image, ensure it is high-quality and optimized for web display.

5. **Layout and spacing:** Adjust the layout and spacing of your header elements using the provided options, such as the logo position, padding, and margins.

As you customize your header, use the live preview to see how your changes will look on desktop and mobile devices. Aim for a design that is clear, visually appealing, and consistent with your overall brand identity.

Best Practices for Header Design

To ensure your header effectively engages your subscribers and reinforces your brand, keep the following best practices in mind:

1. **Keep it simple:** Avoid overcrowding your header with too many elements or information. Focus on the most important aspects of your brand and content, and use whitespace to create a clean, uncluttered design.

2. **Prioritize readability:** Choose fonts and colors that are easy to read and provide sufficient contrast. Avoid using too many different fonts or colors, which can make your header look cluttered and unprofessional.

3. **Optimize for different devices:** Ensure your header looks and functions well on both desktop and mobile devices. Test your design on different screen sizes and email clients to identify any issues with layout, spacing, or responsiveness.

4. **Maintain consistency:** Use consistent branding elements, such as your logo, colors, and fonts, across all your marketing channels to create a cohesive and recognizable brand experience.

5. **Reflect your brand personality:** Use your header design to communicate your brand's unique personality and style. Whether you're aiming for a sleek and professional look or a fun and quirky vibe, ensure your header aligns with your overall brand identity.

Remember, your header is an extension of your brand and a key opportunity to engage your subscribers. By customizing your header to be visually appealing, on-brand, and optimized for different devices, you'll create a strong first impression that sets the stage for a successful newsletter experience.

4.3 Typography and Readability Tips

The typography you choose for your Substack newsletter plays a crucial role in creating a pleasant reading experience for your subscribers. Effective typography enhances readability, conveys your brand personality, and helps guide readers through your content. In this section, we'll explore key considerations for selecting fonts and ensuring readability in your newsletter design.

Choosing Fonts

When selecting fonts for your newsletter, consider the following factors:

1. **Legibility:** Choose fonts that are easy to read at various sizes and on different devices. Sans-serif fonts, such as Arial, Helvetica, or Open Sans, are generally considered more legible on screens than serif fonts.

2. **Brand personality:** Your font choices should align with your brand's personality and style. For example, a sleek, modern font may be appropriate for a tech focused newsletter, while a more traditional serif font may suit a literary publication.

3. **Consistency:** Use a consistent set of fonts throughout your newsletter to create a cohesive and professional look. Avoid using too many different fonts, which can make your design appear cluttered and disjointed.

4. **Hierarchy:** Use different font sizes, weights, and styles to establish a clear hierarchy of information in your newsletter. For example, use a larger, bolder font for headlines and a smaller, regular font for body text.

5. **Web-safe fonts:** If you're not using a custom font, choose web-safe fonts that are likely to be available on most of your subscribers' devices. This ensures that your newsletter will display as intended for all readers.

Substack offers a range of pre-designed font pairings that are optimized for readability and visual appeal. To access these options:

1. Navigate to the "Design" tab in your Substack settings.

2. Scroll down to the "Typography" section.

3. Choose from the available font pairings or select "Custom" to upload your own fonts.

When selecting custom fonts, ensure that you have the necessary licenses and that the fonts are optimized for web use.

Ensuring Readability

In addition to choosing appropriate fonts, there are several other factors that contribute to the readability of your newsletter:

1. **Font size:** Use a font size that is easy to read on various devices. Substack recommends a body font size of 16-18 pixels for optimal readability.

2. **Line spacing:** Adjust the line spacing, or leading, to create a comfortable amount of vertical space between lines of text. A line spacing of 1.5 times the font size is generally considered optimal for readability.

3. **Line length:** Limit the length of your lines of text to around 60-75 characters per line. Longer lines can be difficult to read and follow, while shorter lines can create a choppy reading experience.

4. **Paragraph spacing:** Use sufficient spacing between paragraphs to visually separate distinct ideas and make your content easier to scan. Substack automatically adds a default amount of paragraph spacing, but you can adjust this in the "Typography" section of your design settings.

5. **Text alignment:** Use left-aligned text for your body content, as this is the most natural and readable alignment for longer passages. Avoid fully justified text, which can create awkward spacing and make your content more difficult to read.

6. **Color contrast:** Ensure sufficient color contrast between your text and background to enhance readability. Dark text on a light background is generally the most readable combination.

By carefully considering these factors and making appropriate adjustments in your Substack design settings, you can create a newsletter that is visually appealing, easy to read, and optimized for subscriber engagement.

Testing and Refining Your Typography

As with other aspects of your newsletter design, it's essential to test and refine your typography choices based on subscriber feedback and engagement data. Consider the following strategies:

1. **Seek feedback:** Ask a sample of your subscribers for their opinions on your newsletter's readability and visual appeal. Use this feedback to identify areas for improvement and make adjustments accordingly.

2. **Monitor engagement:** Use Substack's analytics tools to track key engagement metrics, such as open rates, click-through rates, and read times. If you notice a decline in engagement, consider whether your typography choices may be a contributing factor.

3. **Experiment with variations:** Try out different font pairings, sizes, and spacing to see how they impact your newsletter's performance. Use A/B testing to compare the effectiveness of different typography variations and identify the optimal combination for your audience.

Remember, the goal of effective typography is to create a seamless, enjoyable reading experience that keeps your subscribers engaged and coming back for more. By prioritizing readability, brand alignment, and continuous refinement, you can use typography to elevate your newsletter design and build a stronger connection with your audience.

4.4 Using Visual Elements Effectively

While well-crafted text is the foundation of your Substack newsletter, incorporating visual elements can significantly enhance your content's impact and engagement. Effective use of images, graphics, and other visual aids can break up long blocks of text, reinforce key messages, and create a more enjoyable reading experience for your subscribers. In this section, we'll explore best practices for incorporating visuals into your newsletter design.

The Benefits of Visual Elements

Including visual elements in your newsletter offers several key benefits:

1. **Increased engagement:** Visuals can help capture your readers' attention and keep them engaged with your content. Studies have shown that articles with images receive up to 94% more views than those without.

2. **Improved comprehension:** Visual aids, such as infographics or charts, can help simplify complex information and make it easier for readers to understand and retain key points.

3. **Enhanced branding:** Consistent use of visual elements, such as your logo, brand colors, and imagery style, can reinforce your brand identity and make your newsletter more memorable.

4. **Emotional connection:** Carefully chosen images can evoke emotions and create a deeper connection with your readers, making your content more impactful and shareable.

When incorporating visuals into your newsletter, aim to strike a balance between text and images, ensuring that each visual element serves a clear purpose and enhances the overall reading experience.

Types of Visual Elements

There are several types of visual elements you can incorporate into your Substack newsletter:

1. **Photographs:** High-quality, relevant photographs can help illustrate your content, set the tone, and create an emotional connection with your readers. When using photographs, ensure they are properly licensed and credited.

2. **Illustrations and graphics:** Custom illustrations or graphics can help explain complex concepts, provide visual interest, and reinforce your brand style. Consider working with a designer to create unique visual assets for your newsletter.

3. **Infographics:** Infographics combine data, text, and imagery to convey information in a visually engaging way. They are particularly effective for presenting statistics, processes, or comparisons.

4. **Videos and GIFs:** Embedding videos or animated GIFs can add an interactive element to your newsletter and help explain concepts or provide entertainment value. However, use these sparingly to avoid overwhelming your readers.

5. **Buttons and calls-to-action:** Incorporating visual buttons or calls-to-action can draw attention to important links or

actions you want your readers to take, such as subscribing to your paid tier or sharing your newsletter.

When selecting visual elements, prioritize quality over quantity. A few well-chosen, high-quality visuals will be more effective than a cluttered newsletter filled with mediocre images.

Best Practices for Using Visuals

To ensure your visual elements are effective and enhance your newsletter design, follow these best practices:

1. **Relevance:** Choose visuals that are directly relevant to your content and help illustrate or reinforce your key messages. Avoid generic or unrelated images that may confuse or distract your readers.

2. **Consistency:** Maintain a consistent visual style throughout your newsletter, using images that align with your brand colors, tone, and aesthetic. This helps create a cohesive and professional look.

3. **Placement:** Position your visuals strategically within your content to break up long blocks of text and draw attention to key points. Ensure that the placement of your visuals does not disrupt the flow of your content.

4. **Size and resolution:** Optimize your images for web display, ensuring they are large enough to be clear and impactful but not so large that they slow down your newsletter's loading time. Aim for a resolution of 72 dpi for web-based images.

5. **Alt text and captions:** Always include descriptive alt text for your images to ensure accessibility for readers using screen readers. Consider adding captions to provide additional context or credit for your visuals.

6. **Mobile responsiveness:** Ensure that your visuals are optimized for mobile devices, as many of your subscribers will likely read your newsletter on their smartphones. Test your newsletter on various devices to ensure your visuals display properly.

By following these best practices and carefully selecting visuals that enhance your content, you can create a more engaging, visually appealing newsletter that resonates with your subscribers.

Incorporating visual elements into your Substack newsletter is a powerful way to enhance your content's impact, engagement, and memorability. By understanding the benefits of visuals, selecting appropriate types of visual elements, and following best practices for their use, you can create a newsletter design that effectively balances text and imagery to deliver a compelling reading experience.

Remember to prioritize quality, relevance, and consistency in your visual choices, and continually test and refine your approach based on subscriber feedback and engagement data. With strategic use of visuals, you can elevate your newsletter design and create a stronger connection with your audience.

4.5 Creating a Professional and Appealing Layout

The overall layout of your Substack newsletter plays a crucial role in creating a professional, engaging, and user-friendly reading experience for your subscribers. A well-designed layout not only enhances the visual appeal of your newsletter but also guides readers through your content and encourages them to take desired actions. In this section, we'll explore key principles for creating a professional and appealing newsletter layout.

Balancing Text and Visuals

One of the most important aspects of a successful newsletter layout is achieving a balance between text and visual elements. While your written content is the core of your newsletter, incorporating visuals can help break up long blocks of text, add visual interest, and reinforce key messages. Consider the following tips for balancing text and visuals in your layout:

1. **Use whitespace effectively:** Whitespace, or negative space, is the empty space between elements in your design. Adequate whitespace helps create a clean, uncluttered look and makes your content more readable. Use whitespace around your text and images to give your layout breathing room and guide readers' eyes through your content.

2. **Alternate text and images:** Intersperse your text with relevant images, graphics, or other visual elements to create a more dynamic and engaging layout. Avoid placing all your images at the beginning or end of your newsletter, as this can create an unbalanced and less effective design.

3. **Maintain a consistent visual hierarchy:** Use a consistent hierarchy of headings, subheadings, and body text to organize your content and guide readers through your newsletter. This hierarchy should also extend to your visual elements, with more important or impactful visuals given greater prominence in your layout.

4. **Use visual cues to highlight key information:** Incorporate visual cues, such as bold text, colored backgrounds, or icons,

to draw attention to important information or calls-to-action. However, use these cues sparingly to avoid overwhelming your readers or diluting their impact.

By carefully balancing text and visuals in your newsletter layout, you can create a more engaging and effective design that keeps your subscribers reading and coming back for more.

Ensuring Mobile Responsiveness

With more and more people reading emails on their smartphones and tablets, it's essential to ensure that your newsletter layout is optimized for mobile devices. A mobile-responsive design adapts to different screen sizes and orientations, providing a seamless reading experience for your subscribers, regardless of the device they're using. Here are some tips for creating a mobile-responsive newsletter layout:

1. **Use a single-column layout:** While multi-column layouts can work well on desktop screens, they can be difficult to read on smaller mobile screens. Opt for a single-column layout that stacks your content vertically, making it easy for mobile readers to scroll through your newsletter.

2. **Optimize your images for mobile:** Ensure that your images are sized appropriately for mobile screens and don't slow down your newsletter's loading time. Consider using

responsive images that automatically adjust their size and resolution based on the viewer's device.

3. **Make your text readable on small screens:** Use a font size that is easy to read on mobile devices (typically 14-16 pixels) and provide sufficient line spacing and paragraph margins to improve readability. Avoid using wide blocks of text that require horizontal scrolling on mobile screens.

4. **Use clear, tappable calls-to-action:** Ensure that your calls-to-action, such as buttons or links, are large enough and spaced adequately for mobile users to tap easily. Avoid placing links too close together, as this can lead to accidental clicks.

5. **Test your newsletter on various devices:** Before sending your newsletter, test it on a range of mobile devices and email clients to ensure that your layout displays correctly and functions as intended. Substack provides a mobile preview option in the design settings to help you optimize your layout for mobile screens.

By prioritizing mobile responsiveness in your newsletter layout, you can ensure that your content is accessible and engaging for all your subscribers, regardless of their preferred device.

Conclusion

Creating a professional and appealing layout is essential for delivering an exceptional reading experience to your Substack subscribers. By balancing text and visuals effectively, ensuring mobile responsiveness, and maintaining a consistent visual hierarchy, you can design a newsletter that is both visually engaging and user-friendly.

Remember to continually test and refine your layout based on subscriber feedback and engagement data, and don't be afraid to experiment with different design elements to find what works best for your unique audience and content.

With a well-crafted, professional layout as the foundation of your newsletter design, you'll be well-equipped to build a strong, lasting connection with your subscribers and establish your newsletter as a valuable resource in your niche.

Chapter 5: Building and Engaging Your Audience

With your Substack newsletter set up and your content strategy in place, it's time to focus on the most crucial aspect of your success: your audience. Building and engaging a loyal, enthusiastic readership is the key to creating a thriving, sustainable newsletter business. In this chapter, we'll explore proven strategies for attracting readers, fostering a sense of community, and keeping your audience coming back for more. From leveraging your existing network to harnessing the power of social media and SEO, you'll learn how to grow your subscriber base and create a vibrant, engaged community around your newsletter.

5.1 Initial Promotion Strategies

When you first launch your Substack newsletter, it can feel like you're sending your carefully crafted content out into a vast, empty void. But fear not! There are several effective strategies you can use to kickstart your newsletter's growth and attract your first batch of subscribers. In this section, we'll dive into two key initial promotion strategies: leveraging your existing network and using social media to spread the word.

Leveraging Your Existing Network

One of the most powerful tools you have for promoting your new newsletter is your existing network of personal and professional contacts. These are the people who already know, like, and trust you, making them the perfect audience to tap into as you launch your Substack. Here's how to effectively leverage your network:

1. **Create a targeted contact list:** Start by making a list of everyone in your network who might be interested in your newsletter's topic or niche. This can include friends, family, colleagues, clients, and acquaintances who share your passions or could benefit from your content.

2. **Craft a personalized outreach email:** Write a warm, personalized email to each person on your list, letting them know about your new newsletter and why you think they'd enjoy it. Highlight the unique value your content provides and include a clear call-to-action to subscribe.

3. **Offer a special incentive:** To sweeten the deal and encourage your contacts to subscribe, consider offering a special incentive or bonus for signing up. This could be a

free resource, such as an ebook or template, or an exclusive piece of content that's not available to the general public.

4. **Make it easy to share:** In your outreach email, include pre-written social media posts or email templates that your contacts can use to easily share your newsletter with their own networks. This helps extend your reach beyond your immediate circle and tap into the power of word-of-mouth marketing.

5. **Follow up and stay in touch:** After your initial outreach, follow up with your contacts to thank them for subscribing and encourage them to share their thoughts on your newsletter. Keep them engaged by regularly sharing your latest content and asking for their feedback and ideas.

By leveraging your existing network, you can quickly build a core group of engaged subscribers who are invested in your success and can help spread the word about your newsletter.

Using Social Media for Promotion

Social media platforms like X (formerly Twitter), Facebook, LinkedIn, and Instagram are powerful tools for promoting your Substack newsletter and attracting new subscribers. By consistently sharing your content and engaging with your target audience on these platforms, you can expand your reach and drive traffic back to your newsletter. Here are some tips for effectively using social media for promotion:

1. **Choose the right platforms:** Focus your efforts on the social media platforms where your target audience is most active and engaged. For example, if you're writing a newsletter about B2B marketing, LinkedIn might be your best bet, while a newsletter about cooking and recipes might thrive on Instagram and Pinterest.

2. **Optimize your profiles:** Make sure your social media profiles are up-to-date and optimized to promote your newsletter. Include a clear description of your newsletter's topic and value proposition, along with a prominent call-to-action and link to subscribe.

3. **Share your content regularly:** Each time you publish a new newsletter issue, share a link to it on your social media profiles. Use engaging, eye-catching visuals and compelling copy to entice people to click through and read your content.

4. **Engage with your audience:** Don't just broadcast your own content on social media; take the time to engage with your target audience and build relationships. Respond to comments and questions, join relevant conversations, and

share other people's content that aligns with your newsletter's theme.

5. **Use hashtags and tags:** Incorporate relevant hashtags and tags into your social media posts to make your content more discoverable to people interested in your niche. For example, if you're writing a newsletter about personal finance, you might use hashtags like #moneytips, #financialplanning, or #debtfree.

6. **Run social media ads:** Consider investing in paid social media advertising to reach a wider audience and drive more subscribers to your newsletter. Platforms like Facebook and Instagram offer robust targeting options that allow you to get your content in front of the right people based on their interests, demographics, and behaviors.

7. **Collaborate with influencers:** Identify influencers and thought leaders in your niche who have a large, engaged following on social media. Reach out to them to explore collaboration opportunities, such as guest posting on each other's newsletters or cross-promoting each other's content.

By consistently promoting your newsletter on social media and building relationships with your target audience, you can tap into a vast pool of potential subscribers and significantly grow your readership over time.

Leveraging your existing network and using social media for promotion are two essential strategies for kickstarting your Substack newsletter's growth and attracting your first wave of subscribers. By tapping into the power of personal connections and social proof, you can quickly build a core group of engaged readers who are excited about your content and eager to spread the word.

But remember, building and engaging your audience is an ongoing process that requires consistent effort and experimentation. In the next section, we'll dive deeper into the specific tactics and best practices for promoting your newsletter on different social media platforms, so you can maximize your reach and impact. Stay tuned for more actionable insights and strategies to help you grow your newsletter empire!

5.2 Leveraging Social Media

In today's digital landscape, social media platforms have become indispensable tools for promoting your Substack newsletter and engaging with your target audience. As of 2024, there are over 4.6 billion active social media users worldwide, presenting a vast opportunity for newsletter creators to expand their reach and attract new subscribers. In this section, we'll explore the best platforms for promoting your newsletter and share strategies for creating shareable content that resonates with your audience.

Choosing the Right Social Media Platforms

With numerous social media platforms available, it's essential to focus your efforts on the ones that align best with your niche and target audience. Here are some of the most effective platforms for promoting your Substack newsletter in 2024:

1. **X (formerly Twitter):** X remains a powerful platform for sharing news, insights, and opinions, making it an ideal choice for newsletters focused on current events, politics, or industry-specific topics. With its emphasis on short, snappy content and hashtags, X allows you to join relevant conversations and engage with thought leaders in your niche.

2. **LinkedIn:** If your newsletter targets a professional audience or covers business-related topics, LinkedIn is a must-have platform for promotion. LinkedIn's focus on networking and industry-specific content makes it an excellent place to share your newsletter articles, establish your expertise, and connect with potential subscribers.

3. **Facebook:** Despite the rise of newer platforms, Facebook still boasts over 2.9 billion monthly active users in 2024, making it a valuable channel for newsletter promotion. Facebook's robust advertising options and ability to create dedicated pages for your newsletter make it easy to reach a wide audience and foster a sense of community around your content.

4. **Instagram:** For newsletters that rely heavily on visual content or target younger demographics, Instagram is an essential platform. With its emphasis on eye-catching images and short-form video content, Instagram allows you to showcase your newsletter's personality and engage with your audience in a more creative, informal way.

5. **TikTok:** TikTok has continued to grow in popularity since its explosive rise in 2020, with over 1.5 billion active users in 2024. If your newsletter targets a younger audience or covers topics that lend themselves to short-form video content, TikTok can be a powerful tool for promotion and engagement.

6. **YouTube:** For newsletters that incorporate video content or could benefit from a visual component, YouTube remains the go-to platform. With over 2.3 billion monthly active

users in 2024, YouTube offers a vast potential audience for your newsletter and allows you to create engaging, informative content that complements your written articles.

By focusing your efforts on the platforms that best align with your niche and target audience, you can maximize the impact of your social media promotion and attract a steady stream of new subscribers to your newsletter.

Creating Shareable Content

To effectively leverage social media for newsletter promotion, it's essential to create content that is not only valuable and informative but also highly shareable. When your content is shared by your followers and subscribers, it expands your reach and attracts new readers to your newsletter. Here are some strategies for creating shareable content:

1. **Craft compelling headlines:** Just like with your newsletter articles, your social media posts should feature attention-grabbing headlines that entice people to click through and read more. Use strong, active language and clearly communicate the value or benefit of your content.

2. **Use eye-catching visuals:** Social media is a visual medium, so incorporating high-quality images, infographics, or short video clips into your posts can significantly increase their

shareability. Use visuals that are relevant to your content and capture your audience's attention as they scroll through their feeds.

3. **Provide value and insights:** To encourage sharing, your social media content should offer genuine value to your target audience. Share snippets of your newsletter articles that provide actionable advice, thought-provoking insights, or unique perspectives on topics that matter to your readers.

4. **Leverage trending topics and hashtags:** Keep an eye on trending topics and hashtags related to your niche, and create content that joins these conversations in a relevant, meaningful way. By tapping into current trends and discussions, you can increase the visibility and shareability of your content.

5. **Encourage engagement and discussion:** Social media is a two-way conversation, so encourage your followers to engage with your content by asking questions, soliciting opinions, or creating polls. When your audience feels involved and invested in your content, they're more likely to share it with their own networks.

6. **Collaborate with influencers and thought leaders:** Partnering with influencers or thought leaders in your niche

can significantly boost the shareability of your content. By co-creating content or cross-promoting each other's newsletters, you can tap into new audiences and benefit from the social proof and credibility of established experts.

7. **Optimize for each platform:** Each social media platform has its own unique features, audience preferences, and best practices. To maximize the shareability of your content, tailor your posts to the specific platform you're using. For example, use hashtags on X (formerly Twitter) and Instagram, tag relevant people and pages on Facebook, and create visually appealing graphics for Pinterest.

By consistently creating valuable, shareable content and promoting it across the right social media platforms, you can significantly expand the reach of your Substack newsletter and attract a growing audience of engaged subscribers.

Leveraging social media is a crucial component of building and engaging your Substack newsletter audience. By focusing your efforts on the platforms that best align with your niche and target audience, and consistently creating valuable, shareable content, you can tap into the vast potential of social media to grow your subscriber base and foster a thriving community around your newsletter.

But social media promotion is just one piece of the puzzle. In the next section, we'll explore how you can use search engine optimization (SEO) to attract organic traffic to your newsletter and reach even more potential subscribers. Stay tuned for actionable tips and strategies to help you optimize your content and improve your search engine rankings!

5.3 Optimizing for Search Engines

While social media promotion is a powerful tool for attracting new subscribers to your Substack newsletter, it's not the only way to expand your reach and grow your audience. Search engine optimization (SEO) is another crucial strategy for driving organic traffic to your newsletter and reaching potential readers who are actively searching for content related to your niche. In this section, we'll explore the key principles of SEO and share actionable tips for optimizing your newsletter content for search engines in 2024.

Understanding the Importance of SEO

Search engine optimization is the practice of optimizing your website or content to rank higher in search engine results pages (SERPs) for relevant keywords and phrases. When your newsletter content appears at the top of search results, it's more likely to be discovered and clicked on by potential subscribers who are interested in your niche or topic.

In 2024, SEO is more important than ever for newsletter creators looking to grow their audience and establish their authority in their field. With over 5.8 billion searches performed on Google every day, ranking well in search results can bring a significant amount of organic traffic to your newsletter and help you attract highly targeted, engaged subscribers.

Keyword Research and Optimization

One of the foundational elements of SEO is keyword research and optimization. By identifying the keywords and phrases that your target audience is searching for, and strategically incorporating them into your newsletter content, you can improve your chances of ranking well in search results and attracting relevant traffic to your Substack. Here are some tips for effective keyword research and optimization:

1. **Use keyword research tools:** Tools like Google Keyword Planner, SEMrush, and Ahrefs can help you identify high-volume, relevant keywords related to your niche. Look for keywords with a good balance of search volume and competition, and prioritize those that align closely with your newsletter's focus and target audience.

2. **Incorporate keywords naturally:** Once you've identified your target keywords, incorporate them naturally into your newsletter content, including your headlines, subheadings, and body text. Avoid "keyword stuffing" or forcing keywords where they don't belong, as this can actually hurt your search rankings and turn off readers.

3. **Optimize your metadata:** In addition to your main content, be sure to optimize your newsletter's metadata, including your title tags, meta descriptions, and image alt tags. These elements help search engines understand the context and relevance of your content and can improve your click-through rates from search results.

4. **Use long-tail keywords:** In addition to broad, high-volume keywords, consider targeting long-tail keywords that are more specific to your niche or topic. These longer, more detailed phrases may have lower search volume but often indicate a higher level of intent and can attract more targeted, qualified traffic to your newsletter.

5. **Monitor your rankings and adjust:** Use tools like Google Search Console to monitor your newsletter's search rankings and identify opportunities for improvement. Continuously refine your keyword strategy based on your performance

data and audience insights, and adjust your content accordingly.

By conducting thorough keyword research and strategically optimizing your newsletter content, you can improve your search engine visibility and attract a steady stream of organic traffic to your Substack.

Other SEO Best Practices

In addition to keyword optimization, there are several other SEO best practices that can help improve your newsletter's search engine performance in 2024:

1. **Ensure mobile-friendliness:** With the majority of web traffic now coming from mobile devices, it's crucial to ensure that your newsletter content is optimized for mobile viewing. Use responsive design and test your content on various devices to ensure a seamless reading experience for all users.

2. **Improve page speed:** Search engines prioritize websites and content that load quickly, as this provides a better user experience. Optimize your newsletter images, use caching and minification techniques, and choose a reliable hosting provider to ensure fast loading times for your Substack.

3. **Build high-quality backlinks:** Backlinks from other reputable websites can significantly boost your newsletter's search engine authority and rankings. Focus on creating valuable, shareable content that naturally attracts links, and consider guest posting or partnering with other creators in your niche to build your backlink profile.

4. **Leverage internal linking:** Linking between your own newsletter articles can help search engines understand the structure and context of your content, and keep readers engaged on your Substack for longer. Use descriptive, keyword-rich anchor text and link to relevant articles whenever appropriate.

5. **Publish consistently:** Search engines favor websites and content that are regularly updated and provide fresh, relevant information to users. By maintaining a consistent publishing schedule for your newsletter, you can signal to search engines that your content is current and valuable, and improve your chances of ranking well in search results.

By implementing these SEO best practices alongside your keyword optimization efforts, you can create a comprehensive search engine strategy that drives sustained organic growth for your Substack newsletter.

Optimizing your Substack newsletter for search engines is a powerful way to attract organic traffic, reach new audiences, and grow your subscriber base. By conducting thorough keyword research, strategically optimizing your content, and implementing SEO best practices like mobile-friendliness and consistent publishing, you can improve your search engine visibility and establish your newsletter as a valuable resource in your niche.

5.4 Building a Community Around Your Newsletter

Creating a thriving, engaged community around your Substack newsletter is one of the most rewarding and impactful ways to build a loyal, long-term audience. When your subscribers feel like they're part of a vibrant community, they're more likely to remain engaged with your content, share your newsletter with others, and even become paying members. In this section, we'll explore the key strategies for fostering a sense of community and belonging among your readers, and share tips for creating interactive, engaging content that keeps your audience coming back for more.

The Power of Community

Before we dive into specific tactics, let's take a moment to understand why building a community around your newsletter is so valuable. A strong community provides several key benefits for both you and your subscribers:

1. **Increased engagement:** When your subscribers feel like they're part of a community, they're more likely to actively engage with your content, leaving comments, sharing their own experiences, and participating in discussions. This increased engagement can lead to higher open rates, click-through rates, and overall satisfaction with your newsletter.

2. **Improved retention:** Subscribers who feel a sense of belonging and connection to your community are more likely to stick around for the long haul. They're invested not just in your content, but in the relationships and interactions they've built with you and other readers.

3. **Valuable feedback and insights:** An engaged community provides a wealth of opportunities for gathering feedback, ideas, and insights from your readers. By actively listening to and incorporating your community's input, you can create content that better resonates with their needs and interests, and continuously improve your newsletter over time.

4. **Organic growth:** When your community members feel a strong sense of belonging and value, they're more likely to naturally share your newsletter with their own networks, helping you attract new subscribers through word-of-mouth referrals.

By prioritizing community-building alongside your other growth and engagement strategies, you can create a newsletter that not only informs and inspires your readers but also fosters a deep sense of conncection and loyalty.

Strategies for Building Community

So, how can you go about building a strong, engaged community around your Substack newsletter? Here are some key strategies to implement:

1. **Encourage interaction and discussion:** One of the most effective ways to foster a sense of community is to actively encourage interaction and discussion among your readers. At the end of each newsletter, include a prompt or question that invites readers to share their thoughts, experiences, or questions in the comments section. Respond to comments yourself, and encourage readers to engage with each other's ideas as well.

2. **Create interactive content:** In addition to your regular newsletter content, consider creating interactive elements that encourage participation and engagement. This could include polls, surveys, quizzes, or even interactive challenges or exercises related to your niche. By giving your subscribers opportunities to actively participate and contribute, you help them feel more invested in your community.

3. **Host live events and Q&A sessions:** Hosting live events, such as webinars, Q&A sessions, or even virtual meetups, can be a powerful way to deepen your connection with your community and foster real-time interaction. These events give your subscribers a chance to engage with you directly, ask questions, and connect with fellow community members in a more dynamic, personal setting.

4. **Showcase reader contributions:** Celebrate and showcase your community members' contributions and successes whenever possible. This could include featuring reader comments or stories in your newsletter, sharing user-generated content on social media, or even inviting readers to contribute guest posts or interviews. By highlighting your community members' voices and experiences, you help them feel valued and recognized.

5. **Create exclusive content and perks:** Consider offering exclusive content, resources, or perks for your most engaged community members. This could include bonus newsletter issues, access to a private community forum or Slack channel, or even physical merchandise or discounts on your products or services. By rewarding your most loyal and engaged subscribers, you incentivize ongoing participation and commitment to your community.

6. **Foster a positive, inclusive culture:** Finally, make sure to cultivate a positive, welcoming, and inclusive culture within your community. Set clear guidelines and expectations for respectful communication, and actively moderate comments and discussions to ensure a safe, constructive environment for all members. Lead by example, and consistently reinforce the values and norms that define your community.

By implementing these strategies and continually nurturing your community, you can transform your Substack newsletter from a one-way broadcast into a vibrant, interactive hub of engagement and connection.

5.5 Using Substack's Community Features

Substack offers a range of powerful built-in features designed to help you foster a thriving community around your newsletter. By leveraging these tools effectively, you can create a more interactive, engaging experience for your subscribers, and build a stronger sense of connection and loyalty among your readers. In this section, we'll explore two key community features – discussion threads and subscriber-only content – and share best practices for using them to enhance your community-building efforts.

Discussion Threads

Discussion threads are a fantastic way to encourage interaction and engagement among your subscribers. Located at the bottom of each newsletter post, the discussion thread allows readers to leave comments, ask questions, and engage in conversations with you and other community members. Here are some tips for making the most of this feature:

1. **Encourage participation:** At the end of each newsletter, include a clear call-to-action inviting readers to share their thoughts, experiences, or questions in the discussion thread. Make it easy and enticing for them to participate by posing thought-provoking questions or prompts related to your content.

2. **Respond promptly and thoughtfully:** Make a habit of regularly monitoring and responding to comments in your discussion threads. Show your readers that you value their input by providing thoughtful, substantive responses that further the conversation and demonstrate your expertise and engagement.

3. **Foster a positive, inclusive tone:** Set the tone for your discussion threads by modeling respectful, constructive communication. Encourage your readers to do the same by establishing clear community guidelines and moderating comments as needed to maintain a welcoming, inclusive environment.

4. **Highlight valuable contributions:** When readers share particularly insightful comments or spark interesting discussions, consider highlighting their contributions in your next newsletter. This not only shows appreciation for your active community members but also encourages others to participate and share their own thoughts and experiences.

5. **Use threads to gather feedback and ideas:** Discussion threads provide a wealth of opportunities to gather valuable feedback and ideas from your readers. Actively seek out their input on topics they'd like to see covered,

improvements they'd suggest for your newsletter, or challenges they're facing in your niche. By incorporating their feedback and ideas, you can create content that better resonates with your audience and strengthens their investment in your community.

By actively nurturing and engaging with your discussion threads, you can transform your newsletter from a one-way broadcast into a dynamic, interactive community hub that keeps your readers coming back for more.

Subscriber-Only Content

Another powerful community-building tool offered by Substack is the ability to create subscriber-only content. This feature allows you to offer exclusive posts, resources, or perks to your paying subscribers, incentivizing them to upgrade their subscription and deepening their commitment to your community. Here are some ways to leverage subscriber-only content:

1. **Offer bonus content and resources:** Create exclusive content, such as bonus newsletter issues, in-depth tutorials, or downloadable resources, that are only accessible to your paying subscribers. This extra value not only incentivizes subscriptions but also makes your paying members feel

appreciated and rewarded for their investment in your community.

2. **Host subscriber-only events:** Use the subscriber-only feature to host exclusive live events, such as Q&A sessions, webinars, or virtual meetups, for your paying members. These intimate, interactive experiences can help deepen the sense of connection and belonging among your most committed readers.

3. **Create a private community space:** Consider using subscriber-only posts to create a private community forum or discussion space for your paying members. This exclusive area can foster more in-depth conversations, networking opportunities, and peer support among your most engaged readers.

4. **Provide early access or sneak peeks:** Give your paying subscribers early access to new content, products, or features before they're released to your wider audience. This insider access can make them feel valued and excited about being part of your inner circle.

5. **Offer personalized support or coaching:** For higher-tier subscriptions, consider offering personalized support, feedback, or coaching through subscriber-only posts or

private messaging. This one-on-one attention can be a powerful incentive for readers to upgrade their subscription and invest more deeply in your community.

When creating subscriber-only content, be sure to strike a balance between offering genuine value to your paying members and not alienating your free subscribers. Aim to provide a mix of free and paid content that keeps all your readers engaged and motivated to continue following your newsletter.

Substack's built-in community features, such as discussion threads and subscriber-only content, are powerful tools for fostering engagement, interaction, and loyalty among your readers. By actively nurturing your discussion threads, offering exclusive value to your paying members, and continually seeking out ways to involve and appreciate your community, you can create a vibrant, thriving ecosystem around your newsletter.

- Remember, building a strong community takes time, effort, and genuine care. But by consistently showing up, listening to your readers, and providing value and connection, you can cultivate a group of passionate, invested subscribers who will support and champion your newsletter for the long haul.

5.6 Creating a Feedback Loop

One of the most powerful ways to build a thriving, engaged community around your Substack newsletter is to create a feedback loop with your readers. By actively seeking out and incorporating your audience's input, ideas, and preferences, you can create a virtuous cycle of continuous improvement that keeps your content fresh, relevant, and valuable to your subscribers. In this section, we'll explore the importance of reader feedback and share actionable strategies for gathering and using it to refine your newsletter over time.

The Value of Reader Feedback

Reader feedback is a goldmine of insights and opportunities for newsletter creators. By understanding what your audience loves, struggles with, and wants to see more of, you can tailor your content and community experience to better serve their needs and keep them coming back for more. Here are just a few of the benefits of actively seeking and incorporating reader feedback:

1. **Improved content quality and relevance:** When you know what topics, formats, and styles resonate most with your readers, you can create content that is more engaging, valuable, and shareable. By addressing your audience's real

challenges, questions, and interests, you can establish yourself as a go-to resource and authority in your niche.

2. **Increased reader satisfaction and loyalty:** When your readers feel heard, understood, and valued, they're more likely to feel a strong sense of connection and loyalty to your newsletter. By showing that you care about their opinions and are committed to serving their needs, you can foster a more positive, rewarding relationship with your audience.

3. **Enhanced community engagement:** Asking for and responding to reader feedback sends a clear message that your newsletter is a two-way conversation, not just a broadcast. By inviting your subscribers to share their thoughts and experiences, you create more opportunities for interaction, discussion, and collaboration within your community.

4. **Opportunities for growth and innovation:** Reader feedback can often reveal new ideas, angles, or opportunities that you may not have considered before. By staying open to your audience's suggestions and perspectives, you can identify new ways to expand your content, offerings, or reach, and stay ahead of the curve in your niche.

Now that we've established the value of reader feedback, let's explore some practical strategies for gathering and using it effectively.

Strategies for Gathering Reader Feedback

There are many ways to gather feedback from your newsletter subscribers, ranging from informal check-ins to structured surveys and focus groups. Here are some effective methods to try:

1. **End-of-newsletter prompts:** At the end of each newsletter, include a simple prompt encouraging readers to reply with their thoughts, questions, or suggestions. Keep it open-ended and inviting, such as "Hit reply and let me know what you thought of this issue!" or "What topics would you like to see covered in future newsletters?"

2. **Dedicated feedback surveys:** Periodically send out a dedicated feedback survey to your subscribers, using a tool like Google Forms or SurveyMonkey. Ask specific questions about your content, format, frequency, and overall satisfaction, and provide space for open-ended comments and suggestions.

3. **Social media polls and questions:** Use your social media channels to pose quick polls or questions related to your

newsletter content. This can be a fun, low-pressure way to gather input and engage your followers at the same time.

4. **One-on-one reader interviews:** Reach out to a selection of your most engaged subscribers and invite them to participate in a short feedback interview over phone or video chat. This can provide incredibly rich, detailed insights into your readers' experiences and preferences.

5. **Community discussion threads:** Encourage your subscribers to share their feedback and suggestions in your newsletter's discussion threads. Pose specific questions or prompts related to your content, and actively engage with the responses.

No matter which methods you choose, the key is to make feedback-gathering a regular, ongoing part of your newsletter operation. By consistently seeking out and listening to your readers' input, you can create a culture of continuous improvement and collaboration within your community.

Using Feedback to Improve Your Newsletter

Gathering reader feedback is only half the equation – the real magic happens when you actually use that feedback to make meaningful improvements to your newsletter. Here are some tips for effectively incorporating reader feedback into your content and community strategy:

1. **Identify common themes and priorities:** As you review your reader feedback, look for patterns and recurring themes in their responses. What topics, formats, or features are mentioned most often? What pain points or challenges come up repeatedly? Use these insights to prioritize your content planning and development.

2. **Respond and follow up:** When readers take the time to provide feedback, make sure to acknowledge and respond to their input. Thank them for their suggestions, ask clarifying questions, and let them know how you plan to use their feedback moving forward. This shows that you value their opinions and are committed to acting on them.

Implement changes gradually: ***While it's important to be responsive to reader feedback, be careful not to make too many drastic changes too quickly. Implement improvements gradually, and communicate clearly with your subscribers about any changes and the reasoning behind them.***

3. **Close the loop:** As you make updates and improvements based on reader feedback, be sure to circle back and let your

subscribers know. Highlight specific changes or new features that were inspired by their input, and thank them for their role in shaping your newsletter's evolution. This reinforces the value of their feedback and encourages them to continue providing input in the future.

By creating a robust feedback loop with your readers, you can transform your newsletter into a dynamic, collaborative space that evolves and improves along with your audience's needs and preferences.

Building a thriving newsletter community requires more than just publishing great content – it requires actively engaging with and listening to your readers. By creating a feedback loop that gathers, values, and acts on your subscribers' input, you can foster a deeper sense of investment, loyalty, and collaboration within your audience.

- Remember, your readers are your greatest asset and ally in growing your newsletter business. By treating them as partners in your success and consistently working to serve their needs and preferences, you can create a newsletter that not only informs and inspires but also feels like a true community.

Chapter 6: Monetization Strategies

Congratulations! By this point, you've learned how to create a compelling Substack newsletter, craft engaging content, and build a loyal audience. Now, it's time to explore the exciting world of monetization. Turning your passion project into a profitable venture is a crucial step in ensuring the long-term sustainability and success of your newsletter business. In this chapter, we'll dive into various monetization strategies, from offering free and paid subscriptions to finding sponsors, creating affiliate partnerships, and beyond. Get ready to discover the key to unlocking your newsletter's earning potential and building a thriving, rewarding business.

6.1 Free vs. Paid Subscriptions

One of the most fundamental decisions you'll make when monetizing your Substack newsletter is whether to offer free subscriptions, paid subscriptions, or a combination of both. Each approach has its own advantages and considerations, and the right choice for your newsletter will depend on your niche, audience, and overall business goals. In this section, we'll explore the pros and cons of free and paid subscriptions, and provide guidance on setting the right price for your content.

The Case for Free Subscriptions

Offering a free subscription to your newsletter can be a powerful way to attract a wide audience and build a strong foundation for your business. Here are some of the key benefits of a free subscription model:

1. **Lower barrier to entry**: When your newsletter is free, there's no financial barrier preventing readers from subscribing. This can help you quickly grow your subscriber base and reach a larger audience, which is especially valuable in the early stages of your newsletter journey.

2. **Increased shareability**: Free content is more likely to be shared and recommended by your readers, as there's no cost associated with spreading the word. This organic word-of-mouth marketing can be a powerful driver of growth for your newsletter.

3. **Opportunities for upselling**: By offering a free subscription, you can give readers a taste of your content and build trust and credibility over time. This puts you in a strong position to eventually offer paid subscriptions, products, or services to your most engaged and loyal readers.

4. **Flexibility in monetization**: When your newsletter is free, you have more flexibility to experiment with different

monetization strategies, such as sponsorships, affiliate marketing, or product sales. You can test and refine these approaches without the pressure of delivering paid content right away.

However, it's important to recognize the limitations of a free subscription model. When your content is entirely free, you may struggle to generate significant revenue or create a sustainable business over the long term. You'll need to rely on other monetization strategies to compensate for the lack of subscription income, which can be challenging and time-consuming.

The Case for Paid Subscriptions

Offering paid subscriptions to your newsletter can be a powerful way to generate reliable, recurring revenue and build a sustainable business around your content. Here are some of the key benefits of a paid subscription model:

1. **Predictable income**: When readers pay a recurring subscription fee for your newsletter, you can count on a steady stream of income each month. This predictability can help you plan and invest in your business with greater confidence and stability.

2. **Higher perceived value**: When readers pay for your content, they're more likely to perceive it as valuable and high-quality.

This can lead to greater engagement, loyalty, and advocacy from your subscribers, who feel invested in your success.

3. **Stronger reader relationships**: Paid subscribers often feel a deeper sense of connection and commitment to your newsletter, as they've made a financial investment in your content. This can foster a more engaged and supportive community around your business.

4. **Incentive for quality**: When readers are paying for your newsletter, there's a greater incentive to consistently deliver high-quality, valuable content. This accountability can push you to continually improve and refine your newsletter, leading to a better experience for your subscribers.

Of course, there are also challenges to consider with a paid subscription model. When you put your content behind a paywall, you may experience slower growth in your subscriber base, as the financial barrier can deter some potential readers. You'll need to work harder to demonstrate the value and uniqueness of your content to justify the subscription price.

Setting the Right Subscription Price

If you do decide to offer paid subscriptions, setting the right price is crucial for attracting and retaining subscribers. Here are some factors to consider when determining your subscription price:

1. **Value of your content**: Consider the depth, quality, and uniqueness of your content, and how much value it provides to your target audience. The more valuable and specialized your content, the higher the price you can typically charge.

2. **Frequency of publication**: The frequency of your newsletter can also impact your pricing. If you publish daily or multiple times per week, you may be able to charge a higher monthly price than if you publish less frequently.

3. **Niche and audience**: Consider the pricing norms and expectations within your specific niche, as well as the purchasing power and willingness to pay of your target audience. Some niches may support higher subscription prices than others.

4. **Competitive landscape**: Research the pricing of other newsletters or content products in your niche to ensure that your price is competitive and aligned with market expectations.

5. **Perceived value**: Think about how you can enhance the perceived value of your newsletter through additional features, bonuses, or exclusive content. The more value you can offer, the more you can typically charge.

Ultimately, the right subscription price will depend on a variety of factors unique to your newsletter and audience. Don't be afraid to experiment with different price points and gather feedback from your readers to find the sweet spot that maximizes both your revenue and subscriber satisfaction.

In the next section, we'll explore the power of offering tiered subscriptions, and how creating different subscription levels can help you maximize your revenue potential and cater to the diverse needs and preferences of your audience. Get ready to take your monetization strategy to the next level!

6.2 Offering Tiered Subscriptions

Now that we've explored the pros and cons of free and paid subscriptions, let's dive into a powerful monetization strategy that can help you maximize your revenue potential and cater to the diverse needs of your audience: tiered subscriptions. By offering different subscription levels, each with its own unique features and benefits, you can create a more flexible and appealing monetization model that attracts a wider range of subscribers. In this section, we'll explore the key advantages of tiered subscriptions and provide guidance on creating effective subscription tiers for your Substack newsletter.

The Benefits of Tiered Subscriptions

Tiered subscriptions offer several compelling benefits for both newsletter creators and subscribers:

1. **Increased revenue potential**: By offering multiple subscription tiers at different price points, you can capture a larger share of your audience's willingness to pay. Some readers may be happy to pay a premium for exclusive content or additional perks, while others may prefer a more affordable basic subscription.

2. **Greater flexibility for subscribers**: Tiered subscriptions give your readers more choice and control over their subscription experience. They can select the tier that best aligns with their needs, interests, and budget, which can lead to higher satisfaction and retention rates.

3. **Opportunities for upselling**: When you offer tiered subscriptions, you create a natural pathway for subscribers to upgrade over time. As readers become more engaged with your content and invested in your community, they may be more likely to move up to a higher tier to access additional benefits.

4. **Ability to segment your audience**: Tiered subscriptions allow you to segment your audience based on their

subscription level, which can provide valuable insights into their preferences and behaviors. You can use this information to tailor your content, marketing, and engagement strategies to better serve each segment.

5. **Enhanced perceived value**: By offering a range of subscription options, you can create a sense of exclusivity and enhanced value for your higher-tier subscribers. This can help justify premium pricing and foster a stronger sense of loyalty and commitment among your most engaged readers.

Creating Effective Subscription Tiers

To create effective subscription tiers for your Substack newsletter, consider the following steps:

1. **Identify your audience segments**: Start by analyzing your audience and identifying distinct segments based on their needs, interests, and willingness to pay. Consider factors such as their level of engagement, professional background, or specific content preferences.

2. **Define your value proposition for each tier**: Clearly articulate the unique value proposition for each subscription tier. What specific benefits, features, or content will subscribers at each level receive? Make sure there is a clear

and compelling difference between the tiers to justify the price differences.

3. **Determine your pricing strategy**: Set prices for each tier based on the value you're offering and your audience's willingness to pay. Consider using a "good-better-best" pricing model, with a low-priced entry-level tier, a mid-priced "core" tier, and a premium high-end tier.

4. **Choose your tier names and descriptions**: Select clear, descriptive names for each subscription tier that reflect the key benefits and value proposition. Use compelling descriptions to highlight the features and advantages of each tier, and make it easy for potential subscribers to compare and choose the right option for them.

5. **Continuously evaluate and optimize**: Once you launch your tiered subscriptions, continuously monitor your performance metrics and gather feedback from your subscribers. Use this data to refine your tier structure, pricing, and benefits over time, ensuring that you're always delivering maximum value to your audience.

Here's an example of a tiered subscription structure for a fictional Substack newsletter about personal finance:

Basic Tier ($5/month): Access to the weekly newsletter, including budgeting tips, saving strategies, and debt management advice.

Premium Tier ($15/month): Everything in the Basic Tier, plus exclusive monthly deep-dive articles, access to a private community forum, and a monthly Q&A session with the author.

VIP Tier ($50/month): Everything in the Premium Tier, plus personalized financial coaching, priority email support, and early access to new content and products.

By creating clear, compelling subscription tiers that align with your audience's needs and preferences, you can unlock new revenue streams and build a more sustainable, profitable newsletter business.

Remember, creating effective subscription tiers requires a deep understanding of your audience, a clear value proposition for each tier, and a commitment to continuous optimization and improvement. By staying attuned to your subscribers' needs and delivering exceptional value at every tier, you can build a loyal, engaged community of readers who are invested in your long-term success.

In the next section, we'll explore another key monetization strategy: finding sponsors and creating sponsored content. You'll learn how to approach potential sponsors, craft compelling sponsored content, and build mutually beneficial partnerships that support your newsletter's growth and profitability. Get ready to take your monetization game to the next level!

6.3 Finding Sponsors and Creating Sponsored Content

As your Substack newsletter grows and attracts a loyal audience, you may find yourself presented with exciting new monetization opportunities, such as sponsorships and sponsored content. Partnering with relevant brands and businesses can provide a significant source of revenue for your newsletter, while also offering valuable products, services, or insights to your readers. In this section, we'll explore the key strategies for finding sponsors, creating compelling sponsored content, and building mutually beneficial partnerships that support your newsletter's growth and success.

Identifying Potential Sponsors

The first step in securing sponsorships for your newsletter is to identify potential sponsors that align with your niche, values, and audience. Here are some tips for finding the right sponsors:

1. **Look for brands in your niche**: Start by researching companies and products that are directly related to your

newsletter's topic or industry. These brands are more likely to see the value in partnering with you, as your audience is a natural fit for their offerings.

2. **Consider your audience's interests and needs**: Think about the products, services, or resources that your readers would find valuable or interesting. Look for sponsors that can provide solutions to your audience's pain points or enhance their experience in your niche.

3. **Evaluate potential sponsors' values and reputation**: It's important to partner with sponsors that share your values and have a positive reputation in your industry. Research potential sponsors' track records, customer reviews, and public image to ensure they align with your brand and won't alienate your audience.

4. **Leverage your network**: Reach out to your professional network, including colleagues, mentors, and industry contacts, to see if they have any connections or recommendations for potential sponsors. Personal introductions can be a powerful way to open doors and start conversations with prospective partners.

5. **Attend industry events and conferences**: Participating in industry events, conferences, or trade shows can be a great

way to meet potential sponsors in person and build relationships. Come prepared with a compelling pitch and a media kit that showcases your newsletter's audience, engagement, and value proposition.

Crafting a Compelling Sponsorship Pitch

Once you've identified potential sponsors, the next step is to craft a compelling pitch that demonstrates the value of partnering with your newsletter. Here are some key elements to include in your sponsorship pitch:

1. **Introduction and background**: Start by introducing yourself and your newsletter, including your niche, audience size, and engagement metrics. Highlight any notable achievements or milestones that demonstrate your newsletter's growth and impact.

2. **Value proposition**: Clearly articulate the value that your newsletter can provide to the sponsor. This could include access to a highly targeted, engaged audience, the opportunity to build brand awareness and trust, or the ability to drive sales or conversions through sponsored content or exclusive offers.

3. **Sponsorship packages**: Outline the specific sponsorship packages or opportunities you offer, including the types of

content (e.g., sponsored posts, newsletter ads, social media promotion), the duration of the sponsorship, and the pricing for each package. Be clear about what the sponsor can expect in terms of deliverables, metrics, and reporting.

4. **Case studies or testimonials**: If you have previous sponsorship experience, include case studies or testimonials that demonstrate the success and impact of your partnerships. This social proof can help build trust and credibility with potential sponsors.

5. **Call-to-action**: End your pitch with a clear call-to-action, inviting the potential sponsor to discuss the opportunity further or to request more information. Make it easy for them to take the next step and engage with you.

Creating Effective Sponsored Content

When creating sponsored content for your newsletter, it's essential to strike a balance between promoting the sponsor's brand and providing genuine value to your readers. Here are some best practices for creating effective sponsored content:

1. **Align with your brand and voice**: Ensure that the sponsored content aligns with your newsletter's overall brand, tone, and voice. The content should feel authentic and

cohesive with your regular editorial content, rather than a jarring advertisement.

2. **Provide valuable insights or solutions**: Focus on creating sponsored content that provides real value to your readers, whether it's through educational insights, practical tips, or solutions to common challenges in your niche. The more genuinely helpful the content is, the more positively your audience will respond to the sponsorship.

3. **Be transparent about sponsorships**: Always disclose when content is sponsored, in accordance with advertising regulations and best practices. Use clear labels or disclaimers to ensure your readers understand the nature of the partnership and can make informed decisions about engaging with the content.

4. **Collaborate with the sponsor**: Work closely with the sponsor to understand their goals, key messages, and desired outcomes for the sponsored content. Collaborate to develop content ideas and formats that align with both the sponsor's objectives and your audience's interests.

5. **Monitor and optimize performance**: Track the performance of your sponsored content using metrics such as views, engagement, click-through rates, and conversions.

Use this data to optimize your content strategy and demonstrate the value of the sponsorship to both the sponsor and your audience.

By following these best practices and continually refining your approach, you can create sponsored content that enhances your newsletter's value proposition, diversifies your revenue streams, and helps you build long-term, mutually beneficial relationships with sponsors in your niche.

Finding sponsors and creating sponsored content can be a powerful way to monetize your Substack newsletter and provide additional value to your readers. By identifying the right sponsors, crafting compelling pitches, and developing effective sponsored content, you can unlock new revenue opportunities and take your newsletter business to the next level.

In the next section, we'll explore another monetization strategy: affiliate marketing. You'll learn how to choose relevant affiliate products, integrate affiliate links into your content, and earn commissions by promoting products or services that align with your niche and your audience's needs. Get ready to discover a new way to monetize your newsletter while providing value to your readers!

6.4 Affiliate Marketing

Affiliate marketing is another powerful monetization strategy that can help you generate revenue from your Substack newsletter while providing valuable product or service recommendations to your readers. By partnering with relevant companies and promoting their offerings to your audience, you can earn commissions on each sale or lead generated through your unique affiliate links. In this section, we'll explore the key steps to getting started with affiliate marketing and share best practices for integrating affiliate links into your newsletter content.

Choosing Relevant Affiliate Products

The first step in successful affiliate marketing is to choose products or services that are highly relevant to your niche and your audience's needs. Here are some tips for selecting the right affiliate products:

1. **Align with your niche**: Look for products or services that are directly related to your newsletter's topic or industry. The more closely aligned the products are with your niche, the more likely your audience will be interested in them.

2. **Solve your audience's problems**: Choose affiliate products that address your readers' pain points, challenges, or aspirations. By promoting solutions that genuinely help your

audience, you'll build trust and credibility while increasing the likelihood of generating sales.

3. **Evaluate product quality and reputation**: Only promote products or services that you believe in and would recommend to your friends or family. Research the company's reputation, customer reviews, and product quality to ensure you're promoting offerings that will deliver value to your readers.

4. **Consider your personal experience**: Whenever possible, choose affiliate products that you've personally used and can authentically endorse. Sharing your own experiences and results with a product can be a powerful way to persuade your readers to make a purchase.

5. **Look for high-converting offers**: Evaluate the conversion rates and commission structures of potential affiliate products. While it's important to prioritize relevance and quality, choosing products with a track record of high conversions can help maximize your earning potential.

Joining Affiliate Programs

Once you've identified relevant products or services to promote, the next step is to join their affiliate programs. Here are some common ways to find and join affiliate programs:

1. **Directly through the company**: Many companies have their own in-house affiliate programs that you can join directly through their website. Look for a link to their affiliate or partner program in the website footer or navigation menu.

2. **Affiliate networks**: Affiliate networks like ShareASale, Commission Junction, or ClickBank aggregate multiple affiliate programs in one place, making it easy to find and join programs in your niche.

3. **Referral partnerships**: Some companies may not have a formal affiliate program but are open to referral partnerships. Reach out to the company directly to inquire about potential partnership opportunities and negotiate a custom commission structure.

When joining affiliate programs, be sure to carefully review the terms and conditions, commission rates, cookie durations, and payment thresholds to ensure they align with your expectations and goals.

Integrating Affiliate Links into Your Content

Once you've joined relevant affiliate programs, the next step is to strategically integrate your affiliate links into your newsletter content. Here are some best practices for doing so:

1. **Provide genuine value**: Only promote affiliate products in the context of providing genuine value to your readers. Share your honest opinions, experiences, or comparisons of the products, and focus on how they can benefit your audience.

2. **Use natural, conversational language**: Avoid sounding overly salesy or promotional when discussing affiliate products. Use natural, conversational language that aligns with your newsletter's overall tone and voice.

3. **Disclose your affiliate relationships**: Always be transparent about your affiliate relationships and disclose when you're using affiliate links. This helps build trust with your audience and ensures compliance with advertising regulations.

4. **Vary your link placement**: Experiment with different affiliate link placements, such as in-text links, product images, or call-to-action buttons. Track your click-through rates to see which placements are most effective for your audience.

5. **Offer bonus incentives**: Consider offering bonus incentives or exclusive discounts to your readers for purchasing through your affiliate links. This can help increase conversions and show your audience that you're providing additional value.

Following these best practices and continually refining your affiliate marketing strategy, will help you create a sustainable, passive income stream that complements your other monetization efforts and provides value to your readers.

Affiliate marketing is a powerful way to monetize your Substack newsletter by promoting relevant, high-quality products or services to your audience. By carefully selecting affiliate products, joining reputable affiliate programs, and strategically integrating affiliate links into your content, you can generate additional revenue while providing genuine value to your readers.

Remember, successful affiliate marketing requires a balance of authenticity, transparency, and strategic promotion. Always prioritize your audience's needs and interests, and only promote products that you truly believe in and can stand behind.

6.5 Additional Revenue Streams

While subscriptions, sponsorships, and affiliate marketing are the most common monetization strategies for Substack newsletters, there are several additional revenue streams you can explore to diversify your income and create a more resilient business. In this section, we'll discuss three powerful options: online courses and workshops, digital products, and live events. By incorporating these revenue streams into your newsletter business, you can provide even more value to your audience while increasing your earning potential.

Online Courses and Workshops

One of the most effective ways to monetize your newsletter expertise is by creating online courses or workshops that dive deep into specific topics or skills related to your niche. By packaging your knowledge into a structured, step-by-step format, you can help your readers achieve their goals while generating a significant income stream. Here are some tips for creating successful online courses or workshops:

1. **Identify your audience's learning needs**: Start by assessing your audience's most pressing challenges, questions, or aspirations related to your niche. What skills or knowledge do they need to succeed? What topics do they consistently ask about? Use these insights to guide your course creation process.

2. **Choose a specific, actionable topic**: Narrow down your course topic to a specific, actionable skill or outcome that your audience can achieve by completing your course. Avoid trying to cover too much in a single course; instead, focus on providing deep, comprehensive guidance on a targeted topic.

3. **Develop a clear, structured curriculum**: Break down your course topic into a logical, step-by-step curriculum that guides students from foundational concepts to more advanced applications. Use a variety of learning formats, such as video lessons, written content, quizzes, and assignments, to keep students engaged and reinforce their learning.

4. **Leverage your newsletter audience**: Promote your course or workshop directly to your newsletter subscribers, who are already engaged with your content and primed to learn more from you. Offer exclusive discounts or bonuses to your subscribers to incentivize enrollment and reward their loyalty.

5. **Provide ongoing support and community**: Foster a sense of community and accountability among your course participants by offering ongoing support, such as Q&A sessions, group coaching calls, or a private discussion forum. This added value can help increase course completion rates and generate positive word-of-mouth referrals.

By creating high-quality, targeted online courses or workshops, you can establish yourself as a go-to expert in your niche while providing immense value to your audience and generating a lucrative revenue stream.

Digital Products

Another way to monetize your newsletter expertise is by creating and selling digital products that complement your content and provide additional value to your readers. Digital products can take many forms, such as ebooks, templates, checklists, or resource guides, and can be sold as one-time purchases or recurring subscriptions. Here are some tips for creating successful digital products:

1. **Identify your audience's needs and pain points**: Similar to online courses, start by assessing your audience's most pressing needs, challenges, or desires related to your niche. What tools, resources, or information would make their lives easier or help them achieve their goals more quickly?

2. **Create practical, actionable resources**: Focus on creating digital products that provide practical, actionable value to your readers. Avoid fluff or generic content; instead, offer specific, step-by-step guidance, templates, or tools that your audience can immediately apply to their own lives or businesses.

3. **Ensure high quality and professional design**: Invest time and resources into creating visually appealing, professionally designed digital products that reflect your brand and

expertise. High-quality design can increase perceived value and make your products more desirable to potential buyers.

4. **Offer a range of price points**: Consider offering a range of digital products at different price points to cater to different segments of your audience. For example, you could offer a low-priced ebook as an entry-level product, a mid-priced template pack, and a high-end, comprehensive resource bundle.

5. **Promote your products through your newsletter**: Leverage your newsletter as a primary marketing channel for your digital products. Share snippets of your products' content, offer limited-time discounts, or create a sense of urgency around your product launches to encourage sales.

By creating valuable, niche-specific digital products, you can provide additional resources to your audience while generating passive income that complements your other monetization efforts.

Live Events

Finally, consider hosting live events, such as webinars, workshops, or conferences, as a way to monetize your newsletter expertise and provide unique value to your audience. Live events offer the opportunity to connect with your readers in a more personal, interactive setting, while also generating revenue through ticket sales or sponsorships. Here are some tips for creating successful live events:

1. **Choose a compelling, timely topic**: Select a live event topic that addresses a current challenge, trend, or opportunity in your niche. The more timely and relevant your topic, the more likely your audience will be to attend and engage with your event.

2. **Provide a mix of content and interaction**: Structure your live event to include a mix of informative content, such as presentations or panels, and interactive elements, such as Q&A sessions, group discussions, or networking opportunities. This balance will keep attendees engaged and create a more memorable, valuable experience.

3. **Leverage partnerships and guest speakers**: Consider partnering with other experts or influencers in your niche to co-host or speak at your live event. This can help expand your reach, add credibility to your event, and provide additional value to your attendees.

4. **Offer tiered ticket options**: Provide a range of ticket options at different price points, such as general admission, VIP access, or group discounts. This allows attendees to

choose the level of investment and access that aligns with their needs and budget.

5. **Promote your event through multiple channels**: Leverage your newsletter, social media, and other marketing channels to promote your live event and generate buzz. Offer early bird discounts, share behind-the-scenes previews, or create a sense of exclusivity to encourage ticket sales.

By hosting live events, you can create unique, high-value experiences for your audience while generating significant revenue and establishing yourself as a thought leader in your niche.

Diversifying your revenue streams is a smart strategy for building a sustainable, profitable newsletter business. By incorporating online courses, digital products, and live events into your monetization mix, you can provide even more value to your audience while increasing your earning potential and reducing your reliance on any single income source.

Remember, the key to success with these additional revenue streams is to focus on creating high-quality, niche-specific offerings that address your audience's most pressing needs and desires. By consistently delivering value and leveraging your newsletter as a primary marketing channel, you can build a loyal, engaged customer base that supports your business growth.

In the next chapter, we'll explore advanced growth tactics for your newsletter business, including cross-promotion with other newsletters, utilizing Substack's recommendation feature, and running referral programs.

Chapter 7: Advanced Growth Tactics

Congratulations on making it this far! By now, you've learned the fundamentals of creating, launching, and monetizing your Substack newsletter. But why stop there? In this chapter, we'll dive into advanced growth tactics that can take your newsletter to new heights. From cross-promotion and leveraging Substack's recommendation feature to running referral programs and optimizing your performance, you'll discover powerful strategies to supercharge your growth and build a thriving, engaged audience. Get ready to level up your newsletter game and unlock your full potential as a Substack creator!

7.1 Cross-Promotion with Other Newsletters

One of the most effective ways to grow your Substack newsletter is through cross-promotion with other newsletters in your niche or related fields. By partnering with fellow creators to promote each other's content, you can tap into new audiences, build valuable relationships, and create a rising tide that lifts all boats. In this section, we'll explore the benefits of cross-promotion and share best practices for finding and executing successful collaboration opportunities.

The Power of Cross-Promotion

Cross-promotion is a mutually beneficial marketing strategy where two or more newsletter creators agree to promote each other's content to their respective audiences. This can take many forms, such as:

1. **Newsletter swaps**: Each creator includes a mention or excerpt of the other's newsletter in their own newsletter, along with a call-to-action to subscribe.

2. **Guest posts**: Creators write original content for each other's newsletters, providing value to a new audience while also promoting their own newsletter.

3. **Social media shoutouts**: Creators share each other's newsletter content on their social media channels, exposing their partner's brand to a wider audience.

4. **Bundled promotions**: Creators team up to offer a joint promotion, such as a discounted subscription bundle or a giveaway that requires subscribing to both newsletters.

By engaging in cross-promotion, you can enjoy several key benefits:

1. **Increased exposure**: Cross-promotion allows you to reach a new, targeted audience that is likely to be interested in your content. By tapping into your partner's subscriber base, you can quickly and efficiently grow your own audience.

2. **Boosted credibility**: When another respected creator in your niche endorses your newsletter, it lends credibility and social proof to your brand. This can help you attract more subscribers and establish yourself as a trusted authority in your field.

3. **Strengthened relationships**: Collaborating with other creators helps you build valuable relationships and expand your network within your niche. These connections can lead to future opportunities, such as joint ventures, referrals, or even friendships.

4. **Shared workload**: Cross-promotion allows you to share the workload of content creation and marketing with your partner. By dividing tasks and leveraging each other's strengths, you can save time and energy while still achieving your growth goals.

Finding the Right Cross-Promotion Partners

To maximize the impact of your cross-promotion efforts, it's essential to choose the right partners. Here are some tips for finding and vetting potential collaborators:

1. **Look for complementary niches**: Seek out newsletters that cover topics related to your niche but aren't direct competitors. For example, if you write a newsletter about vegan cooking, a newsletter about sustainable living or fitness could be a good fit.

2. **Evaluate audience alignment**: Consider the demographics, interests, and values of your potential partner's audience. Are they similar to your own target audience? Would they be likely to enjoy and benefit from your content?

3. **Assess brand compatibility**: Make sure your potential partner's brand voice, values, and quality standards are compatible with your own. You want to ensure that any content you promote aligns with your brand and resonates with your audience.

4. **Consider audience size**: While it's not always necessary to find partners with the same audience size as you, it's important to ensure that the cross-promotion will be mutually beneficial. Look for partners with engaged audiences that can help you reach your growth goals.

5. **Reach out personally**: When approaching potential partners, take the time to craft a personalized, thoughtful message that demonstrates your familiarity with their work and explains why you think a collaboration would be valuable for both parties.

Best Practices for Successful Cross-Promotion

Once you've found the right partners, follow these best practices to ensure a successful cross-promotion experience:

1. **Set clear goals and expectations**: Before you begin, have an open conversation with your partner about your goals, expectations, and desired outcomes for the collaboration. Make sure you're both on the same page about what success looks like.

2. **Create high-quality, relevant content**: Whether you're writing a guest post, crafting a newsletter swap, or creating social media content, make sure it's your best work. Provide genuine value to your partner's audience and showcase your unique voice and expertise.

3. **Be generous and reciprocal**: Cross-promotion is a two-way street. Be generous with your promotion of your partner's content, and make sure you're both putting in equal effort to support each other's growth.

4. **Track and analyze your results**: Use unique tracking links or codes to measure the impact of your cross-promotion efforts. Analyze metrics like click-through rates, new subscriber numbers, and engagement to evaluate the success of your collaboration and identify areas for improvement.

5. **Nurture your relationships**: Don't view cross-promotion as a one-time transaction. Take the time to build genuine, long-term relationships with your partners. Check in regularly, share updates and successes, and look for ways to support each other's growth beyond the initial collaboration.

By embracing the power of cross-promotion and following these best practices, you can unlock a valuable growth channel for your Substack newsletter and build a supportive network of fellow creators in your niche.

7.2 Utilizing Substack's Recommendation Feature

Substack's recommendation feature is a powerful tool that can help you attract new subscribers and grow your audience organically. When your newsletter is recommended by Substack, it appears in the "Discover" section of the platform, exposing your content to a wider audience of engaged readers. In this section, we'll explore how the recommendation feature works and share strategies for maximizing its benefits for your newsletter growth.

Understanding Substack's Recommendation Algorithm

Substack's recommendation algorithm is designed to surface high-quality, engaging newsletters to readers based on their interests and reading habits. While the exact details of the algorithm are not public, there are several key factors that are known to influence a newsletter's chances of being recommended:

1. **Subscriber growth**: Newsletters that are consistently gaining new subscribers are more likely to be recommended, as this indicates that the content is resonating with readers.

2. **Engagement**: Newsletters with high open rates, click-through rates, and reader interactions (such as comments and likes) are more likely to be recommended, as this suggests that the content is valuable and engaging.

3. **Publishing frequency**: Newsletters that publish consistently and frequently are more likely to be recommended, as this demonstrates a commitment to providing regular value to subscribers.

4. **Topic relevance**: Substack aims to recommend newsletters that are relevant to a reader's interests, based on the other newsletters they subscribe to and engage with.

By focusing on creating high-quality, engaging content and building a loyal subscriber base, you can increase your chances of being recommended by Substack's algorithm.

Optimizing Your Newsletter for Recommendations

To maximize your chances of being recommended by Substack, there are several strategies you can implement:

1. **Encourage subscriber engagement**: Actively encourage your subscribers to open your emails, click on links, leave comments, and like your posts. The more engagement your newsletter receives, the more likely it is to be recommended. Consider using clear calls-to-action, asking questions, or creating interactive content to boost engagement.

2. **Maintain a consistent publishing schedule**: Stick to a regular publishing schedule that your subscribers can rely on. Whether you publish daily, weekly, or monthly, consistency is key to building trust and demonstrating your commitment to providing value.

3. **Use relevant tags and categories**: When setting up your newsletter, be sure to select relevant tags and categories that accurately describe your content. This helps Substack's algorithm understand your newsletter's topic and target audience, increasing the likelihood of being recommended to readers with similar interests.

4. **Collaborate with other Substack creators**: Engage with other Substack creators in your niche or related fields. Leave thoughtful comments on their posts, share their content, and look for opportunities to collaborate or cross-promote. Building relationships with other creators can lead to organic recommendations and increased visibility for your newsletter.

5. **Leverage Substack's features**: Take advantage of Substack's built-in features, such as discussion threads, subscriber-only content, and the "Like" button. These features encourage engagement and help showcase the value and interactivity of your newsletter to potential subscribers.

Maximizing the Benefits of Recommendations

When your newsletter is recommended by Substack, it's essential to capitalize on the increased visibility and potential for new subscribers. Here are some tips for making the most of a recommendation:

1. **Ensure your landing page is optimized**: Make sure your newsletter's landing page is engaging, informative, and optimized for conversion. Use compelling headlines, clear descriptions of your newsletter's value proposition, and strong calls-to-action to encourage visitors to subscribe.

2. **Offer a compelling lead magnet**: Consider offering a free resource, such as an ebook, template, or course, to incentivize new subscribers from your recommended traffic. This lead magnet should provide immediate value and showcase the quality and expertise of your newsletter.

3. **Engage with new subscribers**: When you gain new subscribers from a recommendation, make a point to welcome them personally and encourage them to engage with your content. Respond to their comments, ask for their feedback, and make them feel like valued members of your community.

4. **Analyze and adapt**: Use Substack's analytics tools to track the performance of your newsletter after a recommendation. Analyze metrics like new subscriber numbers, open rates, and engagement to understand what's working and what can be improved. Adapt your content and strategies based on these insights to continue growing your audience.

By optimizing your newsletter for recommendations and maximizing the benefits of increased visibility, you can leverage Substack's recommendation feature to supercharge your newsletter growth and reach new heights of success.

Substack's recommendation feature is a powerful tool for growing your newsletter audience organically. By understanding how the recommendation algorithm works and implementing strategies to optimize your newsletter for recommendations, you can increase your chances of being discovered by new readers and building a thriving subscriber base.

Remember, the key to success with recommendations is consistently creating high-quality, engaging content that resonates with your target audience. By focusing on providing value, encouraging engagement, and building relationships with your subscribers and fellow creators, you can unlock the full potential of Substack's recommendation feature and take your newsletter growth to new levels.

In the next section, we'll explore another effective growth tactic: running referral programs. You'll learn how to incentivize your existing subscribers to refer their friends and colleagues to your newsletter, creating a viral growth engine that can rapidly expand your audience

7.3 Running Referral Programs

Referral programs are a powerful way to tap into the power of word-of-mouth marketing and incentivize your existing subscribers to become advocates for your newsletter. By offering rewards or incentives for referring new subscribers, you can create a viral growth engine that rapidly expands your audience and builds a loyal community around your brand. In this section, we'll explore the benefits of referral programs and share best practices for setting up and running a successful referral campaign for your Substack newsletter.

The Benefits of Referral Programs

Referral programs offer several key benefits for newsletter growth:

1. **Increased trust and credibility**: When a recommendation comes from a trusted friend or colleague, it carries more weight than a cold outreach or advertisement. Referrals from satisfied subscribers lend credibility and social proof to your newsletter, making it more likely that new readers will subscribe and engage with your content.

2. **Cost-effective acquisition**: Referral programs can be a cost-effective way to acquire new subscribers, as you only pay for successful referrals. This can be more efficient than other

paid acquisition channels, such as social media advertising or sponsored content.

3. **Improved subscriber quality**: Referred subscribers are often more engaged and loyal than those acquired through other channels. They have a personal connection to your brand through the friend or colleague who referred them, which can translate into higher open rates, click-through rates, and lifetime value.

4. **Viral growth potential**. A well-designed referral program can create a viral growth loop, where each new referred subscriber is incentivized to refer even more people to your newsletter. This snowball effect can lead to exponential growth and help you scale your audience quickly.

Setting Up Your Referral Program

To set up a successful referral program for your Substack newsletter, follow these steps:

1. **Define your referral incentives**: Decide on the rewards or incentives you'll offer to subscribers who refer new readers to your newsletter. This could be a discount on their subscription, exclusive content or resources, or even physical products or experiences related to your niche. Make sure

your incentives are compelling enough to motivate subscribers to take action.

2. **Choose your referral platform**: Substack doesn't have a built-in referral system, so you'll need to use a third-party platform to manage your referral program. Popular options include ReferralCandy, Viral Loops, and Friendbuy. These platforms provide customizable referral templates, tracking and analytics, and automated reward fulfillment.

3. **Set your referral goals and budget**: Determine how many new subscribers you aim to acquire through your referral program, and set a budget for referral incentives. Make sure to factor in the lifetime value of a referred subscriber when calculating your budget, as this will help you determine the ROI of your referral campaign.

4. **Create your referral messaging**: Craft clear, compelling messaging around your referral program, highlighting the benefits for both the referrer and the referred subscriber. Use strong calls-to-action and make it easy for subscribers to understand how the program works and what they need to do to participate.

5. **Integrate your referral program with your newsletter**: Add referral CTAs and links to your newsletter template,

making it easy for subscribers to refer friends and colleagues directly from your emails. You can also promote your referral program on your website, social media channels, and other marketing materials.

Best Practices for Running Your Referral Program

To maximize the success of your referral program, keep these best practices in mind:

1. **Promote regularly**: Don't just launch your referral program and forget about it. Promote it regularly to your subscribers through your newsletter, social media, and other channels. Consider running limited-time referral bonuses or contests to create urgency and incentivize participation.

2. **Make sharing easy**: Provide pre-written referral messages and social media posts that subscribers can easily share with their networks. The easier you make it for subscribers to refer others, the more likely they are to participate.

3. **Recognize and reward top referrers**: Celebrate and showcase your top referrers, giving them special recognition or additional rewards for their efforts. This can help create a sense of competition and motivation among your subscribers to refer even more people.

4. **Monitor and optimize**: Use your referral platform's analytics and tracking tools to monitor the performance of your referral program. Track metrics like referral conversion rates, reward redemption, and overall ROI. Use these insights to optimize your messaging, incentives, and targeting over time.

5. **Combine with other growth tactics**: Referral programs work best when combined with other growth tactics, such as content marketing, social media promotion, and SEO. Use your referral program as part of a holistic growth strategy to maximize your newsletter's reach and impact.

By implementing a well-designed referral program and following these best practices, you can turn your existing subscribers into powerful growth advocates and rapidly scale your newsletter audience.

Referral programs are a highly effective way to grow your Substack newsletter by leveraging the power of word-of-mouth marketing. By incentivizing your subscribers to refer their friends and colleagues, you can tap into a cost-effective, high-quality acquisition channel that builds trust and loyalty for your brand.

Remember, the key to a successful referral program is to offer compelling incentives, make sharing easy, and consistently promote and optimize your program over time. By combining referral marketing with other growth tactics and delivering exceptional value to your subscribers, you can create a viral growth engine that takes your newsletter to new heights.

7.4 Analyzing and Optimizing Performance

As a Substack newsletter creator, it's essential to continuously monitor and optimize your newsletter's performance to ensure long-term growth and success. By tracking key metrics, using analytics tools, and making data-driven decisions, you can identify areas for improvement, refine your content strategy, and ultimately deliver a better experience for your subscribers. In this section, we'll explore the importance of performance analysis and share best practices for tracking and optimizing your newsletter's key metrics.

Key Performance Metrics to Track

To effectively analyze and optimize your newsletter's performance, you need to track the right metrics. Here are some of the most important metrics to monitor:

1. **Subscriber growth**: Keep a close eye on your subscriber numbers, tracking both new subscribers and unsubscribes

over time. Look for patterns and trends in your growth rate, and aim to maintain a steady, positive trajectory.

2. **Open rates**: Your open rate indicates the percentage of subscribers who open your newsletter emails. A high open rate suggests that your subject lines and preview text are compelling and that your subscribers are engaged with your content.

3. **Click-through rates**: Click-through rates (CTR) measure the percentage of subscribers who click on links within your newsletter. A high CTR indicates that your content is relevant and valuable to your audience, and that your calls-to-action are effective.

4. **Engagement metrics**: Track metrics like comments, likes, and shares to gauge how actively your subscribers are engaging with your content. High engagement levels are a strong indicator of a loyal, invested audience.

5. **Conversion rates**: If you offer paid subscriptions or other products, track your conversion rates to understand how effectively your newsletter is driving revenue. Look for opportunities to optimize your sales funnel and improve your conversion rates over time.

6. **Referral metrics**: If you're running a referral program, track the number of referrals generated, the conversion rate of referred subscribers, and the overall ROI of your referral efforts.

By regularly monitoring these key metrics, you can gain valuable insights into your newsletter's performance and identify areas for improvement.

Using Analytics Tools

To track and analyze your newsletter's performance metrics, you'll need to use analytics tools. Substack provides built-in analytics that allow you to monitor your subscriber growth, open rates, and click-through rates directly from your dashboard. However, you may also want to use additional third-party tools to gain deeper insights and track metrics that Substack doesn't cover. Here are some popular analytics tools to consider:

1. **Google Analytics**: Google Analytics is a free, powerful tool that allows you to track website traffic, user behavior, and conversion rates. By integrating Google Analytics with your Substack newsletter, you can gain insights into how subscribers interact with your content and identify opportunities for optimization.

2. **UTM parameters**: UTM parameters are tags that you can add to your newsletter links to track the source, medium, and campaign of your traffic. By using UTM parameters, you can determine which channels and campaigns are driving the most subscribers and revenue for your newsletter.

3. **Email marketing tools**: If you're using an email marketing tool like Mailchimp or ConvertKit in addition to Substack, you can use their built-in analytics to track metrics like open rates, click-through rates, and subscriber growth.

4. **Social media analytics**: If you're promoting your newsletter on social media, use each platform's built-in analytics tools to track the performance of your posts and identify which types of content resonate best with your audience.

By leveraging a combination of Substack's built-in analytics and third-party tools, you can gain a comprehensive view of your newsletter's performance and make data-driven decisions to optimize your growth and engagement.

Making Data-Driven Decisions

Once you've tracked your key metrics and analyzed your performance data, it's time to turn those insights into action. Here are some tips for making data-driven decisions to optimize your newsletter:

1. **Identify trends and patterns**: Look for patterns in your data, such as a sudden drop in open rates or a spike in unsubscribes. Try to identify the root causes of these trends, such as a change in your content strategy or a technical issue with your emails.

2. **Test and iterate**: Use your performance data to inform your content and marketing experiments. For example, if you notice that certain types of subject lines generate higher open rates, test more variations of those subject lines to optimize your performance.

3. **Segment your audience**: Use your subscriber data to segment your audience based on factors like engagement levels, interests, or demographics. By tailoring your content and messaging to specific segments, you can improve your relevance and engagement.

4. **Prioritize high-impact optimizations**: Focus your optimization efforts on the areas that will have the greatest impact on your newsletter's growth and revenue. For example, if your conversion rates are low, prioritize optimizing your sales funnel over tweaking your email design.

5. **Continuously monitor and adjust**: Performance optimization is an ongoing process, not a one-time event. Continuously monitor your metrics, test new optimizations, and adjust your strategy based on your results.

By making data-driven decisions and continuously optimizing your newsletter's performance, you can unlock new levels of growth, engagement, and revenue for your Substack business.

Analyzing and optimizing your newsletter's performance is a critical component of your long-term success as a Substack creator. By tracking key metrics, using analytics tools, and making data-driven decisions, you can gain valuable insights into your audience's behavior and preferences, and continuously refine your content and marketing strategies to better serve their needs.

7.5 Conducting A/B Testing

A/B testing, also known as split testing, is a powerful optimization technique that allows you to compare two versions of a newsletter element to determine which one performs better. By conducting A/B tests on your subject lines, content, calls-to-action, and other key components, you can make data-driven decisions that improve your newsletter's engagement, conversion rates, and overall performance.

In this section, we'll explore the basics of A/B testing and share best practices for implementing and analyzing tests for your Substack newsletter.

The Basics of A/B Testing

A/B testing involves creating two versions of a specific element in your newsletter, such as a subject line or call-to-action button. Version A is the control, or the original version, while Version B is the variation, or the new version you want to test. You then send each version to a randomly selected portion of your subscriber list and measure the performance of each version based on a specific metric, such as open rates or click-through rates.

The goal of A/B testing is to identify the version that performs better, so you can implement that version for your entire subscriber list and optimize your newsletter's performance over time. By continuously testing and iterating on different elements of your newsletter, you can create a more engaging, effective, and profitable newsletter that resonates with your audience.

Elements to A/B Test in Your Newsletter

There are several key elements you can A/B test in your Substack newsletter to optimize your performance:

1. **Subject lines**: Test different subject line variations to see which ones generate higher open rates. Try variations in length, tone, personalization, or the inclusion of numbers or emojis.

2. **Preview text**: The preview text is the short snippet of text that appears next to your subject line in a subscriber's inbox. Test different preview text variations to see which ones encourage more opens and clicks.

3. **Content formats**: Test different content formats, such as long-form vs. short-form articles, text-based vs. visual content, or single-topic vs. multi-topic newsletters, to see which formats resonate best with your audience.

4. **Calls-to-action**: Test different calls-to-action (CTAs) to see which ones drive more clicks and conversions. Try variations in CTA placement, wording, color, or design.

5. **Send times**: Test different send times and days to see which ones generate the highest engagement rates. Consider testing morning vs. evening sends, weekdays vs. weekends, or different time zones.

6. **Images and graphics**: Test different images, graphics, or visual styles to see which ones capture your audience's attention and drive more engagement.

By continuously testing and optimizing these key elements, you can create a newsletter that is tailored to your audience's preferences and behaviors, and that maximizes your engagement and revenue potential.

Implementing and Analyzing A/B Tests

To implement an A/B test for your Substack newsletter, follow these steps:

1. **Identify your goal**: Determine what you want to achieve with your A/B test, such as increasing open rates, click-through rates, or conversion rates.

2. **Choose your variable**: Select the element you want to test, such as your subject line or call-to-action.

3. **Create your variations**. Develop two versions of your chosen element, making sure that the variations are distinct enough to generate meaningful results.

4. **Split your audience**: Divide your subscriber list into two randomly selected groups, making sure that each group is large enough to provide statistically significant results.

5. **Send your test**: Send Version A to one group and Version B to the other group, making sure to send both versions at the same time to minimize any external factors that could influence your results.

6. **Analyze your results**: After your test has run for a sufficient period (usually at least 24 hours), analyze your results to determine which version performed better based on your chosen metric.

7. **Implement the winner**: Apply the winning version to your entire subscriber list, and use the insights gained from your test to inform future optimization efforts.

When analyzing your A/B test results, it's important to consider statistical significance to ensure that your results are reliable and not due to random chance. Use A/B testing calculators or tools to determine the statistical significance of your results, and only implement changes based on tests that have reached a high level of significance (usually 95% or higher).

A/B testing is a powerful optimization technique that can help you make data-driven decisions to improve your Substack newsletter's performance. By continuously testing and iterating on key elements like subject lines, content formats, and calls-to-action, you can create a newsletter that is tailored to your audience's preferences and that maximizes your engagement and revenue potential.

Remember, A/B testing is an ongoing process that requires patience, experimentation, and a willingness to learn from your data. By staying committed to testing and optimization, you can build a newsletter that not only grows steadily over time but also delivers exceptional value to your subscribers.

In the next chapter, we'll dive into the daily operations and management of your Substack newsletter business, including streamlining your content creation workflow, managing subscriber interactions, and tracking your performance.

Chapter 8: Daily Operations and Management

Congratulations on making it this far in your Substack newsletter journey! By now, you've learned the essential strategies for launching, growing, and monetizing your newsletter. But as your subscriber base grows and your business evolves, it's crucial to have efficient systems in place for managing your daily operations. In this chapter, we'll dive into the nitty-gritty of running your newsletter business, from streamlining your content creation workflow to managing subscriber interactions and tracking your performance. Get ready to optimize your processes and take your newsletter operations to the next level!

8.1 Content Creation Workflow

At the heart of your Substack newsletter's success is your ability to consistently create high-quality, engaging content that resonates with your audience. But as your newsletter grows and your responsibilities expand, it can be challenging to maintain a steady flow of content while also managing the other aspects of your business. That's where having a streamlined content creation workflow comes in. In this section, we'll explore strategies and tools for optimizing your writing process and ensuring that you can efficiently produce top-notch content on a regular basis.

Developing a Writing Routine

One of the most important aspects of a streamlined content creation workflow is establishing a consistent writing routine. By setting aside dedicated time for writing and making it a non-negotiable part of your schedule, you can ensure that you're consistently making progress on your content goals. Here are some tips for developing an effective writing routine:

1. **Choose your peak creative time**: Identify the time of day when you feel most focused, energized, and creative. This may be early in the morning, late at night, or somewhere in between. Experiment with different writing times to find what works best for you.

2. **Set realistic goals**: Determine how much time you can realistically dedicate to writing each day or week, and set achievable goals based on that time frame. Whether it's writing for an hour a day or completing one article per week, having specific targets will help you stay on track.

3. **Create a distraction-free environment**: Find a quiet, comfortable space where you can write without interruptions.

Turn off notifications on your phone and computer, and use tools like website blockers to minimize online distractions.

4. **Break writing into smaller tasks**: If the thought of writing an entire article feels overwhelming, break the process down into smaller, more manageable tasks. This could include outlining, researching, drafting, editing, and proofreading. Focus on one task at a time to avoid feeling overwhelmed.

5. **Use the Pomodoro Technique**: The Pomodoro Technique involves working in focused, 25-minute intervals (called "Pomodoros"), followed by short breaks. This can help you maintain focus and avoid burnout during longer writing sessions.

By developing a consistent writing routine that works for you, you can make steady progress on your content creation goals and avoid the stress and scramble of last-minute writing.

Batching and Repurposing Content

Another key strategy for streamlining your content creation workflow is batching and repurposing your content. Batching involves creating multiple pieces of content in one sitting, rather than spreading the work out over several days or weeks. This can help you get into a focused writing flow and make the most of your creative energy. Here are some tips for effective content batching:

1. **Plan your content in advance**: Use your editorial calendar to plan out your content topics and themes in advance. This will help you batch related content and ensure that you have a steady stream of ideas to work with.

2. **Dedicate blocks of time to batching**: Set aside specific blocks of time for content batching, such as a few hours on a weekend or a full day once a month. Treat these batching sessions as sacred, non-negotiable time for content creation.

3. **Write in stages**: Rather than trying to complete each article from start to finish, work on multiple articles in stages. For example, you could outline several articles in one session, then draft them in the next, and edit them in a final session.

In addition to batching, repurposing your content can also help you save time and maximize the value of your writing. Repurposing involves taking existing content and adapting it into new formats or platforms. For example, you could:

Turn a long-form article into a series of shorter social media posts

Adapt a written article into a podcast episode or video script

Compile several related articles into an ebook or email course

By repurposing your content, you can reach new audiences, reinforce your message, and get more mileage out of your writing efforts.

Using Writing Tools and Templates

Finally, using the right writing tools and templates can help you streamline your content creation process and ensure consistency in your writing. Here are some tools and templates to consider:

1. **Google Docs or Microsoft Word**: These classic word processing tools offer a range of features for drafting, editing, and collaborating on your writing.

2. **Grammarly or Hemingway Editor**: These editing tools can help you catch grammar and spelling errors, improve your sentence structure, and make your writing more clear and concise.

3. **Evernote or Notion**: These note-taking and organizational tools can help you capture ideas, outline articles, and keep your writing projects organized.

4. **Content templates**: Develop a set of templates for different types of content, such as how-to articles, opinion pieces, or interviews. These templates can include outlines, formatting

guidelines, and prompts to ensure consistency and quality in your writing.

By using these tools and templates, you can streamline your writing process, improve your efficiency, and maintain a high standard of quality in your newsletter content.

Developing a streamlined content creation workflow is essential for consistently producing high-quality content for your Substack newsletter. By establishing a writing routine, batching and repurposing your content, and using the right tools and templates, you can optimize your writing process and make the most of your creative energy.

In the next section, we'll explore best practices for managing your email inbox and engaging with your subscribers. From setting up email filters to crafting personalized responses, you'll learn how to build strong relationships with your readers and keep your newsletter community thriving. Stay tuned!

8.2 Managing Subscriber Interactions

As your Substack newsletter grows, so too will your interactions with your subscribers. From responding to comments and emails to moderating discussions and handling customer service inquiries, managing subscriber interactions is a crucial part of building a thriving newsletter community. In this section, we'll explore best practices and strategies for effectively managing your subscriber interactions and fostering positive relationships with your readers.

Setting Up Email Filters and Templates

One of the first steps in managing subscriber interactions is setting up email filters and templates to help you efficiently handle incoming messages. Here's how to get started:

1. **Create email filters**: Use your email client's filtering tools to automatically sort incoming messages based on specific criteria, such as the sender, subject line, or keywords. For example, you could create filters for comments, customer service inquiries, or collaboration requests, so you can quickly identify and prioritize different types of messages.

2. **Develop email templates**: Create a set of email templates for common types of responses, such as thanking subscribers for their comments, addressing frequently asked questions, or welcoming new subscribers. These templates can save you time and ensure consistency in your communication, while still allowing for personalization.

3. **Use canned responses**: Many email clients, such as Gmail, offer a "canned responses" feature that allows you to save and quickly insert pre-written responses into your emails. Use this feature to streamline your email management and ensure prompt, consistent replies to common inquiries.

By setting up email filters and templates, you can efficiently manage your inbox, prioritize important messages, and ensure timely, professional communication with your subscribers.

Responding to Comments and Emails

Engaging with your subscribers through comments and emails is a powerful way to build relationships, foster loyalty, and gather valuable feedback. Here are some best practices for responding to subscriber interactions:

1. **Be prompt**: Aim to respond to comments and emails within 24-48 hours, or sooner if possible. Prompt replies show that you value your subscribers' input and are committed to providing a high level of engagement and service.

2. **Personalize your responses**: Avoid generic, copy-and-paste responses. Instead, take the time to craft personalized replies that address the specific points or questions raised by each subscriber. Use their name, reference their comment or email, and provide thoughtful, relevant insights or answers.

3. **Encourage further engagement**: Use your responses as an opportunity to encourage further engagement and discussion. Ask follow-up questions, invite subscribers to share additional thoughts or experiences, or suggest related topics or resources they might find valuable.

4. **Handle negative feedback gracefully**: Not all subscriber interactions will be positive. When responding to negative comments or complaints, remain professional, empathetic, and solution-oriented. Acknowledge the subscriber's concerns, apologize if necessary, and offer concrete steps to address the issue or improve their experience.

By consistently responding to comments and emails in a prompt, personalized, and engaging manner, you can build strong, positive relationships with your subscribers and foster a loyal, active community around your newsletter.

Moderating Discussions and Handling Conflicts

As your newsletter community grows, you may encounter situations that require moderation or conflict resolution. Here are some tips for effectively moderating discussions and handling conflicts:

1. **Establish clear community guidelines**: Develop a set of clear, concise guidelines that outline your expectations for respectful, constructive engagement in your newsletter

community. Share these guidelines with your subscribers and consistently enforce them to maintain a positive, inclusive environment.

2. **Monitor discussions regularly**: Keep a close eye on comments and discussions to identify potential issues or conflicts early on. Use moderation tools, such as comment filters or approval systems, to automatically flag or hold potentially problematic comments for review.

3. **Address conflicts promptly and fairly**: When conflicts arise, intervene promptly and impartially. Remind participants of your community guidelines, and calmly and respectfully guide the discussion back to a constructive, respectful tone. If necessary, remove or block subscribers who repeatedly violate your guidelines or engage in harmful behavior.

4. **Encourage respectful debate**: Foster an environment that encourages respectful, thoughtful debate and the exchange of diverse perspectives. Model the type of engagement you want to see, and celebrate subscribers who contribute positively to the community.

By proactively moderating discussions and handling conflicts with fairness, consistency, and respect, you can create a safe, engaging space for your subscribers to connect, learn, and grow together.

Remember, your subscribers are the lifeblood of your newsletter business. By consistently prioritizing their needs, engaging with them authentically, and creating a welcoming, inclusive community, you'll be well on your way to building a loyal, passionate audience that will support you for years to come.

8.3 Performance Tracking

As a Substack newsletter creator, regularly tracking and analyzing your performance is essential for making informed decisions, identifying areas for improvement, and ultimately growing your business. By setting up effective tracking systems and conducting regular performance reviews, you can gain valuable insights into your newsletter's health, engagement, and growth. In this section, we'll explore the key steps for implementing a robust performance tracking process and using data to drive your success.

Setting Up Tracking Systems

The first step in effective performance tracking is setting up the right systems to collect and analyze your data. Here are some key tracking systems to put in place:

1. **Substack Analytics**: Substack provides built-in analytics that allow you to track key metrics such as subscriber growth, open rates, click rates, and revenue. Familiarize yourself with these analytics and regularly review them to understand your newsletter's performance.

2. **Google Analytics**: Integrating Google Analytics with your Substack newsletter can provide even more in-depth insights into your audience's behavior, such as page views, time on site, and referral sources. Set up Google Analytics and link it to your Substack account to access this valuable data.

3. **UTM Parameters**: Using UTM parameters on your newsletter links can help you track the effectiveness of your promotion efforts across different channels, such as social media or guest posts. Implement UTM parameters consistently to gain a clear picture of which channels are driving the most traffic and subscribers.

4. **Referral Tracking**: If you're running a referral program, set up a system to track referrals and their conversion rates. This could involve using unique referral links or codes, and

regularly monitoring the performance of your referral campaigns.

By setting up these tracking systems, you'll have a wealth of data at your fingertips to inform your decision-making and optimization efforts.

Conducting Regular Performance Reviews

With your tracking systems in place, it's important to establish a regular cadence for reviewing and analyzing your performance data. Here's a step-by-step process for conducting effective performance reviews:

1. **Set Review Frequency**: Determine how often you'll conduct performance reviews. This could be weekly, monthly, or quarterly, depending on your newsletter's publishing frequency and growth stage. Stick to a consistent schedule to ensure you're regularly monitoring your progress.

2. **Review Key Metrics**: During each review, dive into your key performance metrics, such as subscriber growth, open rates, click rates, and revenue. Look for trends and patterns over time, and compare your performance to industry benchmarks or your own goals.

3. **Identify Successes and Areas for Improvement**: As you review your metrics, identify areas where you're excelling and areas where you could improve. Celebrate your successes and brainstorm strategies for addressing any challenges or weaknesses.

4. **Analyze Individual Pieces of Content**: Dive deeper into the performance of individual newsletter issues or pieces of content. Identify your top-performing content and try to understand what made it resonate with your audience. Similarly, look for underperforming content and consider how you could improve it or avoid similar issues in the future.

5. **Gather Qualitative Feedback**: In addition to quantitative data, gather qualitative feedback from your subscribers through surveys, comments, or email replies. This feedback can provide valuable insights into what your audience loves about your newsletter and what they'd like to see more (or less) of.

6. **Develop an Action Plan**: Based on your analysis and insights, develop a clear action plan for the coming period. Set specific, measurable goals and outline the strategies and tactics you'll use to achieve them. Make sure your action

plan is realistic and aligned with your overall business objectives.

By conducting regular performance reviews and using data to inform your decisions and strategies, you can continuously improve your newsletter's effectiveness and grow your business with confidence.

Performance tracking is a critical component of running a successful Substack newsletter. By setting up effective tracking systems and conducting regular performance reviews, you can gain valuable insights into your newsletter's health, engagement, and growth, and make data-driven decisions to optimize your content and strategies.

8.4 Essential Tools for Content Management

Running a successful Substack newsletter involves more than just writing great content. It also requires effective content management, from organizing your ideas and drafts to collaborating with team members and streamlining your publishing process. Fortunately, there are a variety of powerful tools and software available to help you manage your content like a pro. In this section, we'll explore some of the most essential tools for content management and how to integrate them with your Substack workflow.

Recommended Tools and Software

Here are some of the top tools and software we recommend for managing your newsletter content:

1. **Notion or Evernote**: These versatile note-taking and organization tools are perfect for capturing ideas, outlining articles, and storing research materials. With features like tagging, search, and collaboration, you can keep all your content assets organized and easily accessible.

2. **Google Docs or Microsoft Word**: These classic word processing tools are still the go-to choice for many writers, thanks to their robust editing, formatting, and collaboration features. Use them to draft and refine your articles before publishing on Substack.

3. **Grammarly or Hemingway Editor**: These writing assistant tools can help you polish your prose and ensure your writing is clear, concise, and error-free. They offer suggestions for grammar, spelling, and style improvements, making your editing process more efficient.

4. **Canva or Adobe Creative Suite**: These design tools are essential for creating eye-catching visuals to accompany your newsletter content. Whether you need to design custom graphics, edit photos, or create infographics, these tools offer a range of templates and features to make your visual content shine.

5. **Trello or Asana**: These project management tools can help you organize your content pipeline, assign tasks to team members, and track progress on your editorial calendar. With features like boards, lists, and due dates, you can ensure a smooth and efficient content creation process.

6. **Slack or Microsoft Teams**: These communication tools are invaluable for collaborating with team members, whether you're brainstorming ideas, providing feedback on drafts, or coordinating publication schedules. With features like channels, mentions, and file sharing, you can keep your team aligned and productive.

By incorporating these tools into your content management workflow, you can streamline your processes, improve your efficiency, and ultimately create better content for your Substack newsletter.

Integrating Tools with Substack

While many of the tools mentioned above are standalone applications, some offer direct integrations with Substack to make your content management even more seamless. Here are a few ways you can integrate your favorite tools with your Substack workflow:

1. **Substack API**: Substack offers an API (Application Programming Interface) that allows developers to build custom integrations between Substack and other tools. If you have coding skills or access to a developer, you can use the API to automate tasks like importing content from Google Docs or syncing your editorial calendar with Trello.

2. **Zapier or IFTTT**: These automation tools allow you to create custom workflows between Substack and hundreds of other apps, without needing to code. For example, you could set up a "zap" that automatically creates a new Trello card whenever you publish a new post on Substack, or an "applet" that saves your published posts to Evernote for easy reference.

3. **Browser Extensions**: Some tools, like Grammarly or Evernote, offer browser extensions that can integrate directly with the Substack editor. This allows you to access their features and suggestions as you write, without needing to switch between applications.

By exploring these integration options and finding the ones that work best for your workflow, you can create a seamless and efficient content management system that supports your Substack newsletter goals.

Effective content management is a critical component of running a successful Substack newsletter. By leveraging the right tools and software, and integrating them with your Substack workflow, you can streamline your processes, collaborate more effectively with your team, and ultimately create better content for your readers.

8.5 Payment Processing and Financial Management

One of the most exciting aspects of running a Substack newsletter is the ability to generate revenue through paid subscriptions. However, with that excitement comes the responsibility of properly managing your payment processing and financial systems. In this section, we'll explore the key considerations for setting up and managing your subscription payments on Substack, as well as best practices for handling your newsletter's finances like a pro.

Choosing a Payment Processor

Substack offers built-in payment processing through Stripe, a leading payment gateway known for its security, reliability, and ease of use. When you enable paid subscriptions on your Substack newsletter, you'll be prompted to create a Stripe account and connect it to your Substack account. This allows Substack to handle the payment processing on your behalf, so you can focus on creating great content and growing your subscriber base.

While Stripe is the default payment processor for Substack, it's important to understand the fees and terms associated with using their service. Stripe charges a standard fee of 2.9% + $0.30 per transaction, which is automatically deducted from your subscription revenue. Additionally, Substack charges a 10% fee on all paid subscriptions, which covers their platform costs and support services.

It's important to factor these fees into your pricing strategy and financial projections, to ensure that you're generating enough revenue to sustain and grow your newsletter business.

Setting Up and Managing Subscription Tiers

Once you've connected your Stripe account to Substack, you can set up your subscription tiers and pricing. Substack allows you to offer both monthly and annual subscription options, as well as the ability to create multiple tiers with different pricing and benefits.

When setting up your subscription tiers, consider the following best practices:

1. **Keep it simple**: Avoid overwhelming your potential subscribers with too many options. Start with one or two tiers, and add more as your newsletter grows and you identify new opportunities for differentiation.

2. **Clearly communicate value**: Make sure each subscription tier clearly communicates the value and benefits subscribers will receive. Use compelling language and bullet points to highlight the key features and advantages of each tier.

3. **Offer annual discounts**: Consider offering a discount for annual subscriptions, to encourage longer-term commitment from your subscribers. This can help improve your cash flow and reduce churn over time.

4. **Test and iterate**: Don't be afraid to experiment with different pricing and tier structures over time. Use your analytics and subscriber feedback to inform your decisions, and be willing to make adjustments as needed to optimize your revenue and growth.

By thoughtfully setting up and managing your subscription tiers, you can create a sustainable and profitable revenue stream for your Substack newsletter.

Managing Taxes and Financials

As a Substack newsletter creator, it's important to understand your tax obligations and develop a system for managing your financials. Here are some key considerations and best practices:

1. **Understand your tax obligations**: Depending on your location and business structure, you may be required to pay income taxes, sales taxes, or other fees on your newsletter revenue. Consult with a tax professional or do your own research to understand your specific obligations and ensure compliance.

2. **Keep accurate records**: Maintain detailed records of your newsletter income and expenses, including subscription revenue, payment processing fees, and any business-related expenses like software subscriptions or marketing costs. Use a spreadsheet or accounting software to track your financials and make tax reporting easier.

3. **Set aside funds for taxes**: As you generate revenue from your newsletter, set aside a portion of your earnings to cover your estimated tax obligations. This can help you avoid

surprises come tax time and ensure that you have the funds available to meet your obligations.

4. **Consider forming a business entity**: Depending on your newsletter's revenue and growth trajectory, you may want to consider forming a formal business entity, such as an LLC or corporation. This can provide liability protection and potential tax benefits, but it's important to weigh the costs and administrative requirements against your specific needs and goals.

By staying organized and proactive about your newsletter's finances, you can ensure the long-term sustainability and profitability of your business.

Managing your payment processing and financials is a critical part of running a successful Substack newsletter. By understanding the fees and terms associated with Substack's payment processing, thoughtfully setting up your subscription tiers, and staying on top of your tax obligations and record-keeping, you can create a sustainable and profitable business model for your newsletter.

Remember, as your newsletter grows and evolves, so too will your financial management needs. Stay informed, seek professional advice when needed, and be willing to adapt your systems and strategies to support your ongoing success.

8.6 Legal and Administrative Considerations

As a Substack newsletter creator, it's essential to understand and address the legal and administrative aspects of running your business. From protecting your intellectual property to ensuring compliance with privacy laws and handling taxes, these considerations may not be the most glamorous part of your job, but they're crucial for mitigating risk and maintaining the long-term health of your newsletter. In this section, we'll explore the key legal and administrative issues you need to be aware of and provide best practices for handling them like a pro.

Copyright and Intellectual Property

One of the most important legal considerations for any content creator is protecting your intellectual property. As a Substack newsletter writer, you automatically own the copyright to your original content as soon as you create it. However, there are steps you can take to further protect your work and enforce your rights:

1. **Include a copyright notice**: Add a clear copyright notice to your newsletter and website, indicating that all content is protected by copyright and cannot be reproduced without permission. A simple notice like "© [Year] [Your Name]. All rights reserved." can help deter infringement.

2. **Register your copyright**: While not required, registering your copyright with the U.S. Copyright Office (or your country's equivalent) provides additional legal protections and makes it easier to enforce your rights in case of infringement.

3. **Monitor for infringement**: Regularly monitor the web for unauthorized use of your content, using tools like Google Alerts or Copyscape. If you discover infringement, send a cease-and-desist letter or file a DMCA takedown notice to have the content removed.

4. **Use clear licensing terms**: If you allow others to use or republish your content, make sure to provide clear licensing terms that outline the conditions and limitations of use. Consider using a Creative Commons license to make your terms easily understandable and standardized.

By taking proactive steps to protect your intellectual property, you can safeguard your hard work and maintain control over how your content is used and shared.

Privacy Policies and Terms of Service

Another important legal consideration for Substack newsletter creators is complying with privacy laws and providing clear terms of service to your subscribers. Here are some key steps to take:

1. **Create a privacy policy**: Develop a clear, comprehensive privacy policy that outlines what personal information you collect from your subscribers, how you use and protect that information, and under what circumstances you may share it with third parties. Make sure your privacy policy complies with relevant laws, such as GDPR or CCPA.

2. **Provide terms of service**: Create a terms of service document that outlines the rules and conditions for using your newsletter and website. This should include details on subscription terms, refund policies, acceptable use guidelines, and any limitations of liability.

3. **Obtain necessary consents**: If you collect personal information from your subscribers, such as email addresses or payment details, make sure to obtain their explicit consent and provide clear options for opting out or updating their preferences.

4. **Keep records of compliance**: Maintain detailed records of your privacy and consent practices, including when and how you obtained consent from subscribers, and any requests for data access or deletion. This can help demonstrate compliance in case of an audit or legal challenge.

By prioritizing privacy and providing clear terms of service, you can build trust with your subscribers and minimize legal risks for your newsletter business.

Handling Taxes and Financials

Finally, as a Substack newsletter creator, it's crucial to understand and comply with your tax obligations and maintain accurate financial records. Here are some key considerations:

1. **Determine your tax obligations**: Depending on your location and business structure, you may be required to pay income taxes, self-employment taxes, or sales taxes on your newsletter revenue. Consult with a tax professional or do your own research to understand your specific obligations.

2. **Keep accurate records**: Maintain detailed records of your newsletter income and expenses, including subscription revenue, payment processing fees, and any business-related expenses. Use a spreadsheet or accounting software to track your financials and simplify tax reporting.

3. **Set aside funds for taxes**: As you generate revenue from your newsletter, set aside a portion of your earnings to cover your estimated tax obligations. This can help you avoid surprises come tax time and ensure that you have the funds available to meet your obligations.

4. **Consider professional help**: As your newsletter business grows, consider working with a bookkeeper or accountant to help manage your financials and ensure compliance with tax laws. They can provide valuable guidance and support, freeing you up to focus on creating great content.

By staying on top of your tax obligations and maintaining accurate financial records, you can ensure the long-term sustainability and profitability of your Substack newsletter business.

Navigating the legal and administrative aspects of running a Substack newsletter can feel overwhelming at times, but by taking proactive steps to protect your intellectual property, comply with privacy laws, and manage your finances, you can minimize risks and set your business up for long-term success.

In the next chapter, we'll dive into real-world case studies and expert insights from successful Substack newsletter creators. From in-depth analyses of what makes their newsletters thrive to practical tips and advice for aspiring writers, you'll gain valuable wisdom and inspiration to help you on your own newsletter journey.

Chapter 9: Case Studies and Expert Insights

Throughout this book, we've explored the strategies, tactics, and best practices for launching, growing, and monetizing a successful Substack newsletter. But what does that success actually look like in practice? In this final chapter, we'll dive into real-world examples and insights from some of the most thriving Substack newsletters out there. From in-depth case studies to exclusive interviews with top creators, you'll gain valuable wisdom and inspiration to help you on your own newsletter journey. Get ready to learn from the best in the business and discover what it truly takes to build a newsletter empire.

9.1 Detailed Case Studies of Successful Substack Newsletters

One of the most powerful ways to learn and grow as a Substack creator is to study the success stories of those who have come before you. By analyzing the strategies, content, and engagement tactics of thriving newsletters, you can gain valuable insights and ideas to apply to your own business. In this section, we'll take a deep dive into three remarkable Substack newsletters, exploring what makes them stand out and the key lessons you can learn from their success.

Case Study 1: "The Dispatch" by Steve Hayes and Jonah Goldberg

"The Dispatch" is a political newsletter that has quickly become a go-to source for conservative news and analysis. Founded by veteran journalists Steve Hayes and Jonah Goldberg, the newsletter has amassed over 100,000 subscribers and generates more than $2 million in annual revenue. So, what's the secret to their success?

1. **Niche expertise**: Hayes and Goldberg are well-known and respected voices in the conservative media landscape. By leveraging their expertise and reputation, they were able to quickly establish credibility and attract a loyal audience.

2. **High-quality content**: "The Dispatch" is known for its in-depth, well-researched articles and commentary. The team invests significant time and resources into creating content that is truly valuable and informative for their readers.

3. **Community engagement**: The newsletter has a highly engaged community of readers who actively participate in discussions and debates. The creators foster this engagement by regularly responding to comments and hosting live events and Q&A sessions.

4. **Diverse revenue streams**: In addition to paid subscriptions, "The Dispatch" generates revenue through advertising, sponsorships, and merchandise sales. This diversified income helps ensure the long-term sustainability and growth of the business.

Case Study 2: "The Profile" by Polina Pompliano

"The Profile" is a weekly newsletter that features in-depth profiles of successful people across various industries. Created by Polina Pompliano, the newsletter has grown to over 50,000 subscribers and has become a must-read for anyone interested in entrepreneurship, leadership, and personal development. Here are some key takeaways from "The Profile's" success:

1. **Consistent format**: Each issue of "The Profile" follows a consistent format, featuring a long-form profile of a notable individual, along with curated links and insights. This consistency helps create a strong brand identity and keeps readers coming back each week.

2. **Compelling storytelling**: Pompliano has a knack for crafting engaging, narrative-driven profiles that go beyond surface-level details. By digging deep into her subjects' lives and experiences, she creates content that is both informative and emotionally resonant.

3. **Strategic partnerships**: "The Profile" has partnered with other popular newsletters and media outlets to cross-promote content and reach new audiences. These partnerships have helped the newsletter grow its subscriber base and establish itself as a trusted brand.

4. **Authentic voice**: Pompliano's writing style is personal, relatable, and authentic. By injecting her own personality and perspective into the newsletter, she creates a strong connection with her readers and builds a loyal community around her brand.

Case Study 3: "The Hustle" by Sam Parr

"The Hustle" is a daily business and tech newsletter that has grown to over 1 million subscribers and $10 million in annual revenue. Founded by Sam Parr, the newsletter has become a go-to source for the latest news, trends, and insights in the startup world. Here are some key factors behind "The Hustle's" incredible success:

1. **Unique voice and tone**: "The Hustle" is known for its witty, irreverent, and often humorous writing style. This unique voice helps the newsletter stand out in a crowded market and creates a strong brand identity that resonates with its target audience.

2. **Valuable curation**: In addition to original content, "The Hustle" curates the most important and interesting stories from around the web. This curation saves readers time and helps them stay informed about the latest developments in their industry.

3. **Referral marketing**: "The Hustle" has a highly effective referral marketing program that incentivizes subscribers to share the newsletter with their friends and colleagues. This word-of-mouth growth has been a key driver of the newsletter's rapid expansion.

4. **Diversified business model**: In addition to paid subscriptions, "The Hustle" generates revenue through advertising, sponsorships, and its own line of physical products. This diversified model helps the business weather economic downturns and ensures long-term stability.

By studying these successful Substack newsletters and identifying the strategies and tactics that have contributed to their growth, you can gain valuable insights and inspiration for your own newsletter journey. Whether it's developing a unique voice, creating high-quality content, or building an engaged community, these case studies offer a roadmap for what it takes to succeed on Substack.

9.2 Insights from Top Substack Creators

While case studies provide valuable insights into the strategies and tactics behind successful Substack newsletters, there's nothing quite like hearing directly from the creators themselves. In this section, we've gathered exclusive insights and advice from some of the most accomplished Substack writers out there. From their biggest challenges and surprises to their top tips for aspiring creators, these expert perspectives will give you a behind-the-scenes look at what it really takes to build a thriving newsletter business.

Expert Insight 1: Lenny Rachitsky, "Lenny's Newsletter"

Lenny Rachitsky is the creator of "Lenny's Newsletter," a weekly publication that covers product management, growth, and career advice. With over 50,000 subscribers and a highly engaged community, Rachitsky has established himself as a go-to resource for aspiring and established product managers alike. Here are some of his top insights for Substack creators:

1. **Focus on providing value**: "The most important thing is to consistently provide value to your readers. Whether it's through actionable advice, unique insights, or entertaining stories, your content needs to be worth your readers' time and attention."

2. **Engage with your community**: "Building a strong community around your newsletter is key to long-term success. Respond to comments and emails, ask for feedback, and create opportunities for your readers to connect with each other."

3. **Experiment and iterate**: "Don't be afraid to try new things and see what works best for your audience. Test different content formats, promotion strategies, and monetization models, and be willing to pivot based on the results."

Expert Insight 2: Anne-Laure Le Cunff, "Maker Mind"

Anne-Laure Le Cunff is the creator of "Maker Mind," a newsletter that explores the intersection of neuroscience, creativity, and entrepreneurship. With a background in both neuroscience and startups, Le Cunff brings a unique perspective to her writing and has built a loyal following of curious, ambitious readers. Here are some of her top tips for Substack creators:

1. **Find your unique angle**: "There are countless newsletters out there, so it's important to find a unique angle or perspective that sets you apart. Lean into your own experiences, expertise, and passions to create content that only you can provide."

2. **Be authentic and vulnerable**: "Readers connect with creators who are authentic and vulnerable. Don't be afraid to share your own struggles, mistakes, and lessons learned. This vulnerability can help build trust and loyalty with your audience."

3. **Prioritize quality over quantity**: "It's better to publish one high-quality, well-researched article per week than to churn out mediocre content every day. Focus on creating content that is truly valuable and informative, even if that means publishing less frequently."

Expert Insight 3: Nathan Baschez, "Divinations"

Nathan Baschez is the creator of "Divinations," a newsletter that explores the future of business, technology, and culture. With a background in startups and a knack for insightful analysis, Baschez has built a dedicated following of forward-thinking readers. Here are some of his top insights for Substack creators:

1. **Embrace your niche**: "Don't try to appeal to everyone. Embrace your niche and go deep on the topics that truly fascinate you. By becoming an expert in a specific area, you can attract a highly engaged, loyal audience."

2. **Leverage your network**: "When you're first starting out, leverage your existing network to spread the word about

your newsletter. Reach out to friends, colleagues, and industry contacts who might be interested in your content and ask them to share with their own networks."

3. **Think long-term**: "Building a successful newsletter business takes time and patience. Don't get discouraged if growth is slow at first. Focus on consistently creating great content and engaging with your audience, and trust that the growth will come over time."

By taking these expert insights to heart and applying them to your own newsletter journey, you can avoid common pitfalls, accelerate your growth, and build a truly impactful and rewarding business on Substack.

Conclusion

Congratulations! You've made it to the end of this comprehensive guide to launching, operating, and growing a successful Substack newsletter business. Throughout these pages, we've explored every aspect of the newsletter creation process, from choosing your niche and crafting engaging content to designing your layout, building your audience, and monetizing your work.

We've delved into advanced growth tactics, daily operations, and the legal and administrative considerations that come with running a newsletter business. We've also studied real-world examples of thriving Substack newsletters and heard directly from top creators about their strategies, challenges, and advice for aspiring writers.

By now, you should have a clear roadmap for turning your passion for writing into a profitable and rewarding business on Substack. But as with any journey, the real learning and growth comes from taking action and putting these insights into practice.

Recap of Key Points

Before we part ways, let's take a moment to recap some of the most important takeaways from this book:

1. **Niche selection is crucial**: Choosing a specific, well-defined niche is essential for attracting a loyal, engaged audience and establishing yourself as an expert in your field.

2. **Quality content is king**: Consistently creating high-quality, valuable content is the foundation of any successful newsletter business. Focus on providing unique insights, actionable advice, and engaging storytelling that resonates with your target audience.

3. **Design matters**: A professional, visually appealing newsletter design can make a big impact on reader engagement and retention. Pay attention to your layout, typography, and visual elements to create a polished, on-brand experience.

4. **Community is key**: Building a strong community around your newsletter is essential for long-term success. Engage with your readers, foster discussions, and create opportunities for interaction and feedback.

5. **Diversify your revenue streams**: While paid subscriptions are the primary monetization model on Substack, exploring additional revenue streams like sponsorships, affiliate marketing, and digital products can help you build a more resilient, profitable business.

6. **Continuous optimization is essential**: Regularly analyzing your performance, conducting experiments, and making data-driven optimizations is crucial for ongoing growth and improvement.

7. **Persistence pays off**: Building a successful newsletter business takes time, effort, and patience. Stay committed to your vision, focus on providing value to your readers, and trust that your hard work will pay off in the long run.

Final Encouragement and Tips

As you embark on your own Substack journey, remember that success looks different for everyone. Whether your goal is to build a full-time income, establish yourself as a thought leader, or simply share your ideas with the world, the most important thing is to stay true to your unique voice and vision.

Don't be afraid to experiment, take risks, and learn from your mistakes. Embrace the challenges and opportunities that come with being a newsletter creator, and never stop striving to improve your craft and serve your audience.

Above all, remember that you have something valuable to share with the world. Your experiences, insights, and perspectives matter, and by putting them out there through your newsletter, you have the power to inform, inspire, and impact the lives of countless readers.

So take a deep breath, trust in yourself, and take that first step towards building your newsletter empire. The world is waiting to hear what you have to say.

Resources for Further Learning

While this book has covered a wide range of topics related to Substack newsletter creation, there's always more to learn. In the appendices, you'll find a glossary of key terms, sample templates and checklists, and a curated list of additional resources and reading to support you on your journey.

From online communities of fellow Substack creators to in-depth articles and courses on writing, marketing, and entrepreneurship, these resources will help you continue to grow and thrive as a newsletter business owner.

Go forth, create, and make your mark on the world through the power of your words and ideas. Your Substack success story starts now.

Appendix A: Glossary of Terms

A/B Testing: A method of comparing two versions of a webpage, email, or other marketing asset to determine which one performs better in terms of engagement, conversions, or other metrics.

Affiliate Marketing: A performance-based marketing strategy in which a business rewards affiliates for each customer brought to the company through the affiliate's own marketing efforts.

Analytics: The systematic computational analysis of data or statistics, often used to track and measure the performance of a website, marketing campaign, or other digital asset.

Bounce Rate: The percentage of visitors who navigate away from a website after viewing only one page, often used as a measure of a website's effectiveness at engaging visitors.

Call-to-Action (CTA): A prompt or button on a website or in an email that encourages the reader to take a specific action, such as subscribing to a newsletter or making a purchase.

Click-Through Rate (CTR): The ratio of users who click on a specific link to the total number of users who view the page, email, or advertisement containing the link.

Content Management System (CMS): A software application or set of tools used to create, edit, manage, and publish digital content, often used for managing website content.

Conversion Rate: The percentage of visitors to a website who complete a desired action, such as making a purchase or subscribing to a newsletter.

Domain: The unique web address of a website, used to identify and locate the site on the internet.

Editorial Calendar: A schedule of planned content for a publication, often used by bloggers, content marketers, and newsletter creators to plan and organize their content in advance.

Engagement Rate: A metric that measures the level of interaction and involvement that a piece of content or a social media account receives from its audience.

Inbound Marketing: A marketing strategy that focuses on attracting customers through relevant and helpful content, rather than interrupting them with traditional advertising.

Keyword: A word or phrase that is used to describe the content of a webpage, often used in search engine optimization (SEO) to help a page rank higher in search results.

Landing Page: A standalone web page, created specifically for a marketing or advertising campaign, designed to convert visitors into leads or customers.

Lead Magnet: An incentive, such as a free ebook, whitepaper, or course, offered to potential customers in exchange for their contact information, often used to build an email list.

Niche: A specific segment of a market or audience, often defined by a particular interest, demographic, or need.

Open Rate: The percentage of subscribers who open a specific email campaign, used as a measure of the effectiveness of an email's subject line and preview text.

Paid Subscription: A business model in which readers pay a recurring fee to access premium content or features, often used by newsletters, magazines, and online publications.

Search Engine Optimization (SEO): The practice of optimizing a website or webpage to increase its visibility and ranking in search engine results pages (SERPs).

Subscriber: A person who has opted-in to receive regular updates, newsletters, or other content from a website or publication.

Unique Selling Proposition (USP): A factor or consideration presented by a seller as the reason that one product or service is different from and better than that of the competition.

User-Generated Content (UGC): Any form of content, such as images, videos, text, or reviews, that is created by users or customers of a brand, rather than by the brand itself.

Value Proposition: A statement that clearly communicates the benefits and value that a product or service provides to its target audience.

Appendix B: Templates and Checklists

Content Planning Template

Use this template to plan and organize your newsletter content:

Date	Topic	Headline	Key Points	Call-to-Action	Status

Newsletter Launch Checklist

Use this checklist to ensure you've covered all the essential steps before launching your Substack newsletter:

[ ] Choose a niche and define your target audience

[ ] Develop your unique value proposition

[ ] Set up your Substack account and customize your profile

[ ] Choose a memorable name and URL for your newsletter

[ ] Design your newsletter template and header

[ ] Create a content plan and editorial calendar

[ ] Write and schedule your first few newsletter issues

[ ] Set up your subscription tiers and pricing (if applicable)

[ ] Integrate your social media accounts and other marketing channels

[ ] Promote your newsletter launch to your existing network and audience

Weekly Newsletter Management Checklist

Use this checklist to stay organized and on track with your weekly newsletter operations:

[ ] Review and update your content plan and editorial calendar

[ ] Research and gather information for upcoming newsletter topics

[ ] Write and edit your newsletter content

[ ] Select and optimize images and other visual elements

[ ] Format and proofread your newsletter for readability and clarity

[ ] Schedule your newsletter for delivery

[ ] Promote your newsletter on social media and other channels

[ ] Engage with your subscribers and respond to comments and emails

[ ] Analyze your newsletter performance and gather feedback

[ ] Plan and implement any necessary improvements or optimizations

Sponsored Content Checklist

Use this checklist to ensure you're creating effective and compliant sponsored content for your newsletter:

[ ] Identify and reach out to potential sponsors that align with your niche and audience

[ ] Negotiate and agree on the terms of the sponsorship, including compensation and deliverables

[ ] Develop a clear and compelling concept for the sponsored content

[ ] Create the sponsored content, ensuring it provides value to your readers and aligns with your brand voice

[ ] Disclose the sponsorship clearly and transparently within the content

[ ] Obtain approval from the sponsor before publishing

[ ] Publish and promote the sponsored content to your audience

[ ] Provide the sponsor with any agreed-upon performance metrics or reports

[ ] Evaluate the success of the sponsored content and gather feedback for future improvements

Monthly Performance Review Template

Use this template to conduct regular performance reviews and track your newsletter's growth and engagement:

Metric	Previous Month	Current Month	Change
Subscribers			
Open Rate			
Click-Through Rate			
Engagement Rate			
Revenue			
Expenses			
Net Profit			

Key Takeaways and Action Items:

-

-

-

-

-

-

-

-

-

Appendix C: Additional Resources and Reading

Recommended Books

1. "The Business of Newsletters" by Simon Owens
2. "Newsletter Marketing Strategies" by Liam Veitch
3. "Email Marketing Rules" by Chad S. White
4. "The Copywriter's Handbook" by Robert W. Bly
5. "Everybody Writes" by Ann Handley
6. "The Elements of Style" by William Strunk Jr. and E.B. White
7. "The Sense of Style" by Steven Pinker
8. "On Writing Well" by William Zinsser
9. "The Storytelling Edge" by Shane Snow and Joe Lazauskas
10. "Made to Stick" by Chip Heath and Dan Heath

Recommended Articles

1. "How to Start a Successful Newsletter" by David Perell

2. "The Ultimate Guide to Growing Your Newsletter" by Steph Smith
3. "How to Create a Newsletter People Actually Read" by Sophia Bernazzani
4. "The Art and Science of Newsletters" by Nisha Chittal
5. "How to Write a Newsletter That People Want to Read" by Ginny Mineo
6. "The Anatomy of a Perfect Newsletter" by Kayla Hollatz
7. "How to Monetize Your Newsletter" by Ethan Brooks
8. "The Power of Email Newsletters" by Kelsey Libert
9. "How to Measure the Success of Your Newsletter" by Jacqueline Kyo Thomas
10. "The Future of Email Newsletters" by Anum Hussain

Online Resources and Tools

1. Substack Resources: https://on.substack.com/resources
2. Substack Writer Office Hours: https://on.substack.com/office-hours
3. Substack Writer Community: https://writers.substack.com/
4. Newsletter Creators Network: https://newslettercreators.com/
5. Newsletter Crew: https://newslettercrew.com/
6. Really Good Emails: https://reallygoodemails.com/

7. Mailchimp Resources: https://mailchimp.com/resources/
8. Campaign Monitor Resources: https://www.campaignmonitor.com/resources/
9. Litmus Resources: https://www.litmus.com/resources/
10. Canva Design School: https://designschool.canva.com/

Online Communities and Forums

1. Substack Writers Facebook Group: https://www.facebook.com/groups/substackwriters
2. Newsletter Nerds Facebook Group: https://www.facebook.com/groups/newsletternerds
3. Newsletter Creators Hub on Slack: https://newslettercreatorsnetwork.com/hub
4. IndieHackers Newsletter Founders Group: https://www.indiehackers.com/group/newsletter-founders
5. r/Newsletters on Reddit: https://www.reddit.com/r/Newsletters/
6. #EmailGeeks on x: https://x.com/hashtag/emailgeeks
7. #NewsletterChat on x: https://x.com/hashtag/newsletterchat
8. Newsletter Creators on LinkedIn: https://www.linkedin.com/groups/13877991/

9. Email Marketing Forum on Quora: https://www.quora.com/topic/Email-Marketing
10. Email Marketing Professionals on LinkedIn: https://www.linkedin.com/groups/2282999/

These additional resources, including books, articles, online tools, and communities, should provide you with a wealth of knowledge and support as you continue your journey as Substack newsletter creator. By exploring these resources and engaging with fellow creators, you can stay up-to-date on industry trends, learn new strategies and tactics, and find inspiration and guidance for growing your newsletter businesses.

Printed in Great Britain
by Amazon